The Heroic Christ

The Heroic Christ

The Hero's Journey in the Gospel of Luke

NICKOLAS A. FOX

Foreword by Brian Zahnd

CASCADE *Books* · Eugene, Oregon

THE HEROIC CHRIST
The Hero's Journey in the Gospel of Luke

Copyright © 2025 Nickolas A. Fox. All rights reserved. Except for brief quotations in critical publications or reviews, no part of this book may be reproduced in any manner without prior written permission from the publisher. Write: Permissions, Wipf and Stock Publishers, 199 W. 8th Ave., Suite 3, Eugene, OR 97401.

Cascade Books
An Imprint of Wipf and Stock Publishers
199 W. 8th Ave., Suite 3
Eugene, OR 97401

www.wipfandstock.com

PAPERBACK ISBN: 979-8-3852-1438-9
HARDCOVER ISBN: 979-8-3852-1439-6
EBOOK ISBN: 979-8-3852-1440-2

Cataloguing-in-Publication data:

Names: Fox, Nickolas A. [author]. | Zahnd, Brian [foreword writer].

Title: The heroic Christ : the hero's journey in the Gospel of Luke / by Nickolas A. Fox ; with a foreword by Brian Zahnd.

Description: Eugene, OR: Cascade Books, 2025 | Includes bibliographical references.

Identifiers: ISBN 979-8-3852-1438-9 (paperback) | ISBN 979-8-3852-1439-6 (hardcover) | ISBN 979-8-3852-1440-2 (ebook)

Subjects: LCSH: Bible.—Luke—Criticism, interpretation, etc. | Jesus Christ—Biography. | Campbell, Joseph, 1904–1987. | Heroes in literature. | Heroes.

Classification: BS2595.2 F69 2025 (paperback) | BS2595.2 (ebook)

VERSION NUMBER 120825

All Scripture quotations, unless otherwise indicated, are taken from the Holy Bible, New International Version®, NIV®. Copyright © 2011 by Biblica, Inc.™ Used by permission of Zondervan. All rights reserved worldwide. www.zondervan.com The "NIV" and "New International Version" are trademarks registered in the United States Patent and Trademark Office by Biblica, Inc.™

Scripture quotations marked KJV are from the King James or Authorized Version.

Scripture quotations marked MSG are taken from THE MESSAGE. Copyright © 2002. Used by permission of NavPress Publishing Group.

Artwork by Megan Phillips.

For June, Brenda, Angela, and AJ
—four particularly heroic females in my life

A hero ventures forth from the world of common day into a region of supernatural wonder: fabulous forces are there encountered and a decisive victory is won: the hero comes back from this mysterious adventure with the power to bestow boons on his fellow man.

—Joseph Campbell, *The Hero with a Thousand Faces*, 31

Contents

List of Illustrations | viii
Foreword by Brian Zahnd | ix
Preface | xiii
Acknowledgments | xv
Abbreviations | xvii

Introduction: The Hero's Journey in Luke | 1

PART 1: DEPARTURE

1. The Mundane World | 17
2. The Call to Adventure | 30
3. Supernatural Aid | 40
4. Crossing the Threshold | 50

PART 2: INITIATION

5. The Hero's Companions | 61
6. The Road of Trials | 69
7. The Journey | 85
8. The Approach: Jesus's Final Week | 97
9. The Ordeal | 107

PART 3: RETURN

10. Resurrection | 121

Bibliography | 133

List of Illustrations

The Departure | 15
The Initiation | 59
The Return | 119
The Hero's Journey in Luke | 131

Foreword

WE HUMANS ARE STORYTELLING, story-loving creatures. We spend a phenomenal amount of our life telling, hearing, reading, and watching stories—from grand epics like *Lord of the Rings* to the mildly interesting anecdote told to coworkers in the office. Hundreds of millions of stories are being told throughout the world at this very moment. It's what we do. Story is not peripheral to human life; it is absolutely central. There's a reason why Homer, Shakespeare, J. R. R. Tolkien, and J. K. Rowling are among the most famous people in history—they rank among our greatest storytellers. Why are Tom Hanks and Meryl Streep so beloved, so well known, and so well compensated? Because they are so gifted and skilled at playing roles in some of our favorite stories. We have an innate love of stories and a remarkable ability to remember stories. If we hear the names Romeo and Juliet or Bonnie and Clyde, a narrative immediately arises in our imagination unbidden. To remember something, all we need do is hear it in the form of a story.

All of this indicates that our love of story comes from a much deeper place than a fleeting desire for a bit of entertainment. Story is the essence of meaning; coherence requires some form of narrative. To avoid the despair that Søren Kierkegaard called "the sickness unto death,"[1] we need to believe that our life is not merely an absurd accident tumbling out of a random assortment of atoms. Furthermore, we need to believe that our life somehow fits into a grand metanarrative—that we are part of a story bigger than ourselves. We all want to belong, to have our part in some Big Story. Absent a metanarrative to interpret our place in history, the yawning abyss of nihilism awaits. Most people would rather cling to any story, even a tragedy, than fall into the dread void of meaninglessness. Storytellers are not mere entertainers; they are evangelists.

---

1. Kierkegaard, *Sickness unto Death*.

Foreword

And this is why post-Enlightenment Christians in the postmodern Western world need to be reminded of the true nature of the gospel: it's a *story!* The gospel is not a set of spiritual laws or abstract theological principles or a series of prescribed steps; the gospel is a story—the story of Jesus Christ. In its most basic form it's the story of Jesus's death, burial, and resurrection. A fuller telling of the story takes us from a manger in Bethlehem to an empty tomb in Jerusalem. The biblical Gospels *are* the gospel. And the director's cut edition is the big story the Bible has to tell—the story that takes us from Genesis to Revelation; from paradise lost to paradise regained; from the alpha of creation to the omega of new creation. When we reduce the gospel to abstract principles or denominational dogmas, the story is lost; and when the story is lost, the audience is lost as well. Dry atonement theories are no substitute for the paschal mystery that transports us from Gethsemane to Golgotha to the garden of Joseph of Arimathea. Either we keep the gospel a story or we make the gospel boring—a grievous sin indeed! A de-storied gospel creates a void that will be filled with other stories—stories of progress, politics, nationalism, or even outrageous conspiracy theories. In a world hungry for stories, Christians need to keep attentively hearing and creatively telling their own story.

In recognizing the gospel as a story, we are not saying the gospel is a *fiction*; rather, we are saying the gospel has a *narrative structure*. The gospel has many antagonists and one great Protagonist; it's full of drama, suspense, intrigue, tragedy, even comedy; and it has the greatest surprise ending of all time. It's good news that the *good news* is a story and not an arcane theological lecture. Abstract theological concepts can be difficult to grasp and retain; but anyone who has heard the parable of the prodigal son even once can remember the basic storyline: two sons, far country, riotous living, hard times, pigpen, journey home, forgiving father, feast of fatted calf . . . but will the other brother come to the party? And if the story is a truly great story, we don't want to hear it just once, we want to hear it again and again. Every Christmas we want to hear the story that begins like this: "And there were in the same country shepherds abiding in the field, keeping watch over their flocks by night" (Luke 2:8 KJV). Every Easter we want to again thrill at the marvelous line, "Why seek ye the living among the dead? He is not here, but is risen" (Luke 24:5–6 KJV).

So along with Homer, Shakespeare, Tolkien, and Rowling, we can add another bard to the pantheon of great storytellers: Luke the Evangelist. Luke tells his two-volume gospel story to Theophilus—the God lover. And

Foreword

whether Theophilus was Luke's patron or Luke's literary device, God lovers for two millennia have remained endlessly fascinated with Luke's telling of the Jesus story—the gospel travel adventure that takes us first from Bethlehem to Jerusalem, and then in the sequel from Jerusalem to Rome.

And though it may be a cliché, the gospel really is the greatest story ever told. It's the greatest story because it is the true story of God creating, loving, and saving the world through Jesus Christ. The gospel is the ultimate story that in one way or another all the great stories are trying to tell or at least point toward. The great stories, myths, and epics intuit something of the gospel story woven into the cosmos. When Joseph Campbell speaks of the hero with a thousand faces, he is recognizing the mythic structure of the hero's journey that becomes true in the face of Jesus Christ.[2] This is the very thing C. S. Lewis recognized about mythic literature just prior to his conversion when another soon-to-be-converted atheist colleague at Oxford said to him, "Rum thing, all that about the Dying God. Seems to have really happened once." Thus C. S. Lewis and Bede Griffiths came to faith in Christ through recognizing the gospel as true myth. And who was their evangelist? None other than the grand storyteller J. R. R. Tolkien.

Now Nickolas Fox has given us a wonderful gift in *The Heroic Christ*. This fascinating book is a Joseph Campbell–informed analysis of the hero's journey in Luke's Gospel that helps us recover the true narrative nature of the good news. As Fox will point out in what follows, he's not looking to Campbell for theological interpretation but for instruction on how to read Luke's Gospel as the great story that it really is. Having carefully read and thoroughly enjoyed *The Heroic Christ*, I'm now eager to return to Luke's Gospel and read it again with new eyes and deeper appreciation. And dear reader, I'm sure this will be true for you as well.

Brian Zahnd
The Feast of Saint Luke

---

2. Campbell, *Hero with Thousand Faces*.

Preface

Art exists that one may recover a sensation of life; it exists to make one feel things, to make the stone stony.
—Viktor Shklovsky, "Art as Technique," 12

A COMMON PROBLEM STUDENTS of the Bible have, particularly concerning the Gospels, is that they become *too* familiar. The stories have been told and retold (and told some more). People who have attended church their whole lives and studied the Bible at undergraduate, graduate, and even doctoral levels risk becoming too comfortable with these stories, something Shklovsky calls *habitualization,* which "devours works, clothes, furniture, one's wife, and the fear of war."[3]

A number of years ago when I was in seminary, I was doing work for an Old Testament class that required me to read some of Robert Alter's book *The Art of Biblical Narrative*. His third chapter, the one on biblical type-scenes, sparked my curiosity like few things up to and since that point in my academic career.[4] Immediately, I began thinking of narrative scenes in the Bible and how they conformed to and deviated from the type-scenes as Alter discussed them. It was a discovery that truly changed the way I think about both narratives and the Bible.

Joseph Campbell's literary model of the Hero's Journey had a similar impact on me, although not as acutely. I do not remember when I first encountered the model, but I am sure it was not from Campbell himself.

---

3. Shklovsky, "Art as Technique," 12. For an interesting engagement with this, see Resseguie, *Narrative Criticism*, 30–38.

4. The full chapter title is "Biblical Type-Scenes and the Uses of Convention."

Preface

Rather, it must have been from the popularity of the model in the ether of modern American storytelling—Hollywood, television, narrative documentaries. Although more of a slow burn, the concept of the Hero's Journey—a remarkably high number of stories from around the globe from time immemorial share similar features—captivated me. For whatever reason, my mind works that way, seeing narrative patterns and examining them. As a Gospels scholar, I started to wonder if the story of Jesus had similar tropes as we see in the Hero's Journey, if we could gain and learn something through applying this model to the life of Jesus. As it turns out, I think we can. This book is an attempt to invigorate that conversation with my students, colleagues, and the academy at large.

What is more, this is a way I have found to stave off Shklovsky's habitualization, to keep the stories fresh.[5] While the stories of Jesus are never dull and lifeless, they can become, at times, rote and overly repeated, needing a fresh perspective and new energy. When we approach the Gospels allowing the power of story to truly speak, exciting things can happen.

Joseph Campbell's Hero's Journey is a way that I have found to make the stone *stony* again. It breathes new life into old forms. It helps us read the stories of Jesus and experience them as art, the sensation of life.

That, dear reader, is what I wish for you to experience in the pages that follow.

May you enjoy the adventure.

N. Fox
September 2024

---

5. Shklovsky would call this *ostraneniye* (making strange).

Acknowledgments

I AM THANKFUL TO so many who assisted in making this work into a reality.

To the God of the story, the original creative who inspires stories the world over.

To my wife Angela, for support and encouragement. The writing of this book coincided with the most stressful period of an eight-and-a-half-year struggle with infertility that resulted in eight trips out of state, untold amounts of money, and the accompanying stress and heartache. And yet, God was with us through it all. Our baby girl, AJ, was born in December. God is good! Thank you, Ang, for your partnership in life and faith.

I am so thankful to Pastor Brian Zahnd, who agreed to write the foreword for this volume. I am honored to share the page with you and collaborate in doing the important work of writing, creating, and telling this most important story.

To the esteemed faculty at Crown College for their friendship and support. I am blessed to have great colleagues. Dr. Don Bouchard and Dr. Ryan Furlong both helped with conversations, ideas, and editing feedback at various points in the project.

To my TA, Kylee Tollefsrud, for administrative support toward the end of the project, and to all my students, past, present, and future.

And to the wonderful people at Cascade Press who made this work possible.

Thank you.

Abbreviations

AB	Anchor Bible
Ann.	*Annales*
Ant.	*The Antiquities of the Jews.* In *The Works of Josephus*, edited by William Whiston, 29–542. Rev. ed. Peabody, MA: Hendrickson, 1998
AYBRL	Anchor Yale Bible Reference Library
BDAG	Danker, Frederick W., et al. *Greek-English Lexicon of the New Testament and Other Early Christian Literature.* 3rd ed. Chicago: University of Chicago Press, 2000 (Danker-Bauer-Arndt-Gingrich)
BECNT	Baker Exegetical Commentary on the New Testament
BRev	*Bible Review*
Fast.	*Fasti*
JBL	*Journal of Biblical Literature*
JSNTSup	Journal for the Study of the New Testament Supplement Series
J.W.	*Jewish War*
LCL	Loeb Classical Library
Legat.	*Legatio ad Gaium*
LNTS	The Library of New Testament Studies
LXX	Septuagint
NICNT	New International Commentary on the New Testament

ABBREVIATIONS

NTS	*New Testament Studies*
SBLSPS	Society of Biblical Literature Seminar Papers
SP	Sacra Pagina
ThTo	*Theology Today*
TS	*Theological Studies*
WBC	Word Bible Commentary
WGRW	Writings from the Greco-Roman World

Introduction
The Hero's Journey in Luke

Myth is the secret opening through which the inexhaustible energies of the cosmos pour into human cultural manifestation.
—Joseph Campbell, *The Hero with a Thousand Faces*, 3

THE 1999 MOVIE *THE Matrix* by the Wachowskis was a game changer for me. The first time I saw it was a special experience. The early intrigue of the world and the confusion—Who are the good guys? Who is the voice on the phone, and why does he know so much? Is his computer alive?—the textures—a cool black-and-green color scheme, leather clothes, trend-transcending sunglasses—and of course the action sequences, supplemented with the best special effects of the time.[1]

But beyond the mystery, the style, the cool music, and the special effects was something deeper that resonated with me. Here we see a normal guy who is not normal. In fact, Neo has a calling on his life. He is taken, plucked from his normal, mundane world in one of the most dramatic crossing-the-threshold scenes in all of cinema, and then must be initiated into the rules of this strange new world. He goes on quests, talks to guides, and fights the enemies, all to culminate in a scene of sacrifice, resurrection, and ultimate hope at the end (I'm speaking in broad terms to avoid spoiling too much, but if you haven't seen *The Matrix* at this point . . .).

1. I have to confess: I did not see the original *Matrix* movie in the theater when it was released. I fell in love with it on the small screen. Happily, while this book was in its final stages *The Matrix* came back to theaters for its twenty-fifth anniversary, and I was able to remedy a missed opportunity from my teen years.

I was aware even back then, as a precocious teenager who loved Jesus and Scripture, that there were significant messianic themes in the movie. What I didn't know until later, though, was how fundamental this framework is in stories told around the world, both ancient and modern. Called the Hero's Journey, it is a framework, the skeleton around which a story can be fleshed out. Being aware of these story elements helped me read biblical narrative—namely, the Gospels—in a new way.

A WORLD OF STORIES

This practice of identifying story motifs is common; we do it subconsciously. There are certain patterns and plot points that we expect to see coming. How many times have you been reading a book or watching a movie and had this sense that said something like "He is going to betray the other guy," or "It's too quiet, something bad is going to happen," or "Those two people are going to fall in love," and you were right? This is for two reasons: (1) humans have a narrative mental substructure that interprets their experiences as stories, and because of this, (2) we live in a world filled with stories. Allow me to briefly comment on each of these.

Many have previously noted the narrative substructure of the human brain, integral to how we think and communicate.[2] This starts from observing how powerful and pervasive stories are in our lives. As Jonathan Gottschall asserts, "We are, as a species, addicted to story. Even when the body goes to sleep, the mind stays up all night, telling itself stories."[3] This internal narrative of human consciousness is backed up by neuroscience as well.[4] We think and live through the lens of stories, so much so that at times our brains confuse random information for intelligent narratives.[5] Suffice it to say here, we experience the world, both individually and collectively, through stories.

---

2. Liu and László, "Narrative Theory," 87.

3. Gottschall, *Storytelling Animal*, xiv. Gottschall's book is a real tour de force in the pervasiveness and power of story in the human life; children and adults, awake or asleep, for better or worse, Gottschall covers it all.

4. Siegel, *Mindsight*.

5. Gottschall tells of scientific experiments that illustrate this point, as well as argues that this overactive desire to see a narrative in everything is how we get conspiracy theories (*Storytelling Animal*, 87–116).

Introduction

This is perhaps best demonstrated by my second point, that we live in a world completely saturated by stories. Everything from movies and TV shows, podcasts, sports, advertisements, and the role you play in your work, family, and social systems have the fundamental elements of story—like characters, plot, and conflict—imbedded in them. The ubiquity of stories dates back thousands of years. While the original readers of the Bible may not have had those media, their lives were filled with narratives nonetheless.

In short, the more we can learn about and understand the way stories and narratives work, the better we will be at engaging with and interpreting those narratives. Enter Joseph Campbell.

THE CONTRIBUTIONS OF JOSEPH CAMPBELL

With regard to the analysis of stories throughout history, Joseph Campbell was a formidable figure. A literature professor by trade, he was a gifted student, both in formal education and from his personal research. He was a vociferous reader of stories from around the world from a young age. Already a published author several times over, his major contribution came in 1949 when his book *The Hero with a Thousand Faces* was published. In this seminal work, Campbell pulled together streams and characteristics from stories around the world and throughout time and created what he called the Hero's Journey, a framework observable in a staggeringly high number of stories told and recorded in human history.[6]

Over the next decades, Campbell's book and his ideas became more and more influential. Authors and filmmakers took notice and would use Campbell's Hero's Journey to create their own stories. Perhaps the most famous example of this is George Lucas in writing the screenplay of *Star Wars*. Lucas would call Campbell "my Yoda," and the Hero's Journey would become a staple for Hollywood screenwriters.[7] Numerous books have been published since then, and the Hero's Journey motif has become part of the common lexicon of storytelling.[8]

---

6. Campbell actually first called it the Adventure of the Hero, but the more popular title would soon catch on (*Hero with a Thousand Faces*, 47).

7. Bancks, "Beyond the Hero's Journey," 34.

8. Vogler, *Writer's Journey*; Soloponte, *Ultimate Hero's Journey*; Murdock, *Heroine's Journey*. Another reason Campbell became something of a household name was the interview series he did with Bill Moyers on PBS in 1988 called *Joseph Campbell and the*

The Heroic Christ

Some may think Campbell an odd choice to assist us with reading and interpreting the New Testament, for Campbell had a complicated relationship with organized religion. While he was raised Catholic, he distanced himself from the church in his adult life. He was more scientifically minded than religiously minded, particularly when it comes to the historicity of the story. And he was at times quite critical of the church and organized religion. And yet, he is a mystic. He understands the need for stories that give meaning to the lives of humans. Indeed, he declares that when societies lose these meaning-making stories, the ones that give us morality and creativity, the result is disequilibrium, leaving us with "nothing firm to hold onto."[9] While we don't look to Campbell to be our expert historian or orthodox theologian, he has a worthwhile contribution to make in the way we read and examine stories. I trust that my readers, like my students, can set aside some ideological differences with Mr. Campbell in order to see the great contribution he brings to the craft of reading narratives and connecting the dots.

Stories are something of a universal language among humans. It is not unlike a Christian and an atheist who go to see a film together at the local cineplex. Afterwards, perhaps they go to a local establishment and, over appetizers and drinks, share how they were both inspired by the film's contributions to life, hope, and goodness. The Christian may notice messianic themes that remind her of sacrifice and salvation. The atheist may recognize those same themes, or he may connect with the endurance of the characters through hardship, connected with a deep humanism, allowing them to come out stronger on the other end. In this give-and-take of different perspectives and ideas, both are better for it. In the same way, an open-minded reader can engage with Campbell and be inspired as we learn about stories and story framework together.[10]

In scholarly terms, what I am doing is a form of narrative criticism. Broadly speaking, narrative criticism "attends to the literary and storied qualities of a biblical narrative, like a Gospel."[11] In addition, I am taking

---

Power of Myth. These interviews were turned into a book (Campbell, *Power of Myth*). And a great modern look at the Hero's Journey is presented in the Netflix documentary *Myths and Monsters*, directed by William Simpson.

9. Campbell, *Myths to Live By*, 10.

10. The Christ story—as well as the images that go with it—remains one of Campbell's most referenced narratives (Campbell, *Thou Art That*, xii).

11. Brown, *Gospels as Stories*, 11. See also Brown, "Narrative Criticism"; Resseguie, *Narrative Criticism*, 17–21.

INTRODUCTION

something of a literary criticism approach as well, as I seek to use the tools we use to evaluate literature and apply them to the story of the Gospels.[12] It seems to me that Campbell's story motif is significantly helpful, and we would do well to see how it might help us read the Gospels better.

THE DEFINITION OF MYTH

One of the most important terms used by Campbell in his writing is the word "myth" or its other form, "mythology." This word comes with a fair amount of modern baggage, so understanding what he means—and does not mean—by the word is very important.[13] Indeed, I beg of the reader not to stumble over this word. Campbell does not use myth pejoratively. Rather, he speaks of myth as the significant power that a story has.

To define myth from Campbell's writings is a bit daunting—not because Campbell doesn't define it but because he says so much about myth and mythology in different volumes over different decades that pulling all the information together is a challenge. Put in a single sentence from Campbell's own writing, *mythology* is "an organization of symbolic images and narratives, metaphorical of the possibilities of human experience and the fulfillment of a given culture at a given time."[14] He says later that these images give the person "a sense of participation in a field of meaning."[15] From these two brief statements, a number of elements rise to importance. First, myths are all about the symbols and the narratives. Campbell's best work will focus primarily on those symbolic elements (e.g., the hero, the threshold, the belly of the whale, etc.). Second, myths arise from cultures, from a group of humans in a time and place. Understanding time and place is important to understand the story, but conversely, engaging with the story can help us understand the time and place. To understand the biblical story, we need to know the context from which it is told. Last, and most important, myths allow humans to engage with and participate in meaning.

Is there anything more essential to human survival and human flourishing than a healthy sense of meaning? The enemy in our disenchanted age is nihilism. That is what fuels chaos and violence. Nihilism comes from

---

12. Resseguie, *Narrative Criticism*, 19.

13. A good look into the history and etymology of this word and how we arrived at the modern situation of confusion is Doty, "Myth Around the Clock."

14. Campbell, *Thou Art That*, 1–2.

15. Campbell, *Thou Art That*, 8.

lacking an organizing metanarrative, an overarching story that gives purpose, meaning, and direction to our lives and existence. Meaning charges humans with an important place in the cosmos. Stories help us counter the nihilism in our hearts and minds in order to grasp something essential and true—our meaning and our existence. Thus, there is an existential stream in this process of reading stories through the lens of Campbell. Although stories may be entertaining, they are ultimately about much more, connecting us with what it means to be human, how to live out our values, and how to leave this world better than we found it.[16]

Four Functions of Myth

Another elaboration on mythology may be helpful. Campbell elucidates four functions of myths that are worth our consideration here. First, myths reconcile us to the awe-inspiring universe—the *mysterium tremendum*. Have you ever read or heard a good story that left you with an overwhelming sense of clarity of what was good, true, and important in the world? Even in harsh, gritty contexts, stories can remind us both that reality is amazing and that we have a part to play in that.

Second, myths serve an interpretive function, "to present a consistent image of the order of the cosmos."[17] Human minds do well with order. When reality has a structure to it, it allows us to make sense of complex relationships. While, like anything, creating a prescribed cosmic order can be abused, it is fundamental to the nature of narrative worlds.

Third, myths "validate and support a specific moral order."[18] One can easily see how this is related to the previous point. Once one has an image of the structure of the cosmos, that person must know the rules of interaction, the morality of the system. This is why we tell children stories that have moral takeaways. Some, myself included, can grow frustrated with children's Bibles that ignore many key stories in the text because they don't easily lend themselves to an obvious moral payoff that is easily graspable by children. The ones that do are smoothed out and simplified. While my love for the nuance and complexity in the biblical text is valid, I must

---

16. For a fuller discussion on why humans tell stories, see Storr, *Science of Storytelling*, 11–17.

17. Campbell, *Thou Art That*, 3.

18. Campbell, *Thou Art That*, 5.

acknowledge that I understand why we do this. Children need morality presented to them through stories.

Finally, the fourth function of myths is "to carry the individual through the various stages and crises of life—that is, to help person's grasp the unfolding of life with integrity."[19] When I was in high school, a new follower of Jesus looking to navigate the complexities of the teenage social experience, there arose the popularity of bracelets with the letters WWJD (What would Jesus do?). For a couple years of my life, you could hardly find me without one of these on my wrist. It allowed me, when I was facing a temptation, a tough decision, or social pressure, to access the narratives and examples of Jesus and his character—as well as those of my pastors and faith community—to assist me in my crisis. While that may seem cheesy to some, I can attest to the power that being reminded of those stories and relational connections has on a person, and furthermore, I suspect we all do this in different ways, harnessing different narratives, characters, and values.

Campbell offers a helpful analogy of a baby kangaroo—a joey. A joey is in the womb of its mother only three weeks.[20] It emerges from the womb into the pouch, where it will stay for much longer while it grows and develops. He humorously calls this "a womb with a view."[21] Humans, too, he contends, are born into the pouch of stories for the first twelve years of our lives. We need these stories and these myths—the symbolic images and narratives—to help us make sense and meaning of our lives, the world around us, and the social setting we find ourselves in. What a beautiful picture of the meaning-making stories in the lives of young people! However, that process does not stop at twelve years old. One of Campbell's critiques of organized religion is that he feels it tries to keep people in the pouch of childhood stories their whole lives, even when they have matured beyond it.[22] While there are certainly childhood stories that should be abandoned with maturity—the tooth fairy and Santa Clause come to mind—does the story of Jesus stop being inspirational in middle school? Does loving your

---

19. Campbell, *Thou Art That*, 5.

20. Depending on the kind of kangaroo, modern science suggests that it ranges from twenty-eight to thirty-three days, so four to five weeks. Nonetheless, Campbell's analogy still works.

21. Campbell, *Myths to Live By*, 216.

22. Campbell, *Myths to Live By*, 216–17. Campbell is not uniform in his critique here. He certainly does not believe myths or meaning-making stories are only for children. But he does make that strong point about religion here, and I differ with him on that point.

enemy and being challenged by Jesus's prophetic call and sacrificial death wane in adolescence? By stark contrast, it is at this point where the true nature of Jesus and his mission, his sacrifice, his wisdom, begins to make fuller sense. In a time when the young person begins to question what they are to do in this crazy world, what their gifts are, who they are in their family, and who they are called to be when they transition out of their family is when the challenge of Jesus to our selfish egos and plans is sorely needed. Lest we ever grow up and leave these stories behind, we instead engage more deeply with their wisdom and calling on our lives.

READING DIFFERENTLY

Think about how you read the Bible compared to how you read a fictional novel. In the novel, you focus on the story, you notice character development throughout, you lose yourself in the world the author is creating for you. This experience has been described as "abductive" (contrasted with inductive or deductive), in that you are abducted by the story into new and marvelous lands.[23] Now compare that to the way many people read the Bible, particularly the Gospels. You read a story, an encounter that Jesus has with another person, or one of his teachings. You reflect on it and let it teach you; maybe you meditate on how you can apply this to your life. You might read in the notes in your Bible about the location of this particular encounter or who the political leader was at the time. This may precede a time of prayer. All of this is fine, but it is much different than your experience with the novel, where you lose yourself in the narrative. Mincing the Gospels into daily bite-sized chunks robs them of the larger narrative.[24] You miss out on a certain degree of fascination that the novel gave you. And while the Gospels are not modern fiction novels, they do share some of those same elements: setting, story, characters, tension and conflict, climax. It matters little that the New Testament is a narrative rooted in history and the novel is purely fiction. Our brains want to engage the story in each case. So why do we read the Bible so differently?

In her book *Re-Enchanting the Text: Discovering the Bible as Sacred, Dangerous, and Mysterious*, Cheryl Bridges Johns uses the phrase *pneumatic imagination*, that is, when the Spirit "actively employs the human

---

23. Sweet et al., *A is for Abductive*, 31–33.
24. For more on this critique, see Brown, *Gospels as Stories*, 3–4.

Introduction

imagination" in reading Scripture.²⁵ Imagine the impact of combining the power of the Holy Spirit engaging your imagination with the natural captivating power that comes from story. That is how we should read the Gospels: inspired by the Spirit and engaged with the story of the narrative.²⁶ That is a life-giving approach that helps us make transcendent meaning in our lives. To that end, I think applying the template of the Hero's Journey to the Gospel stories can help us engage our storied imaginations as we encounter the life of Jesus.

Let me give you a personal story from my life as an example. My maternal grandmother, June, was the spiritual matriarch of our family, and she lived an inspiring life of courage, love, and strength for her family. The youngest of twelve children, all born on the back porch of a small house in a small town in central Illinois, she had a father who was an alcoholic and a loving mother who was a do-it-all woman with a pioneering spirit. June would take after her mother in this way. After her mother's death when June was sixteen, she would marry a kind factory worker. She gave birth to her first child at seventeen and two more in the next few years. During this time, her kind factory worker husband started to drink and became mean. She says the first time he was abusive was the day she told him she wanted to be baptized—he didn't want her making herself better than him. The physical abuse continued for several years until one night she had had enough. As she was putting her three kids to bed, she told her oldest son, "Go ahead and get in bed, but keep your jeans on. I will be back in a few minutes." She went and lay in bed with her husband. A little while later, she said, "I think I hear the baby fussing." She went down the hall, told her son to help get his little brother ready, while she got the baby's stuff together. They quietly snuck out of the house and loaded into the car. Their one car started only about 50 percent of the time. June said a prayer, "God, please help me. If this car doesn't start, I'm dead." The car started on the first try. June didn't drive, but that day, resourceful and pioneering as she was, she figured it out. As she was backing out of the driveway, her husband, having heard the car start, came to the door and shaking his fist yelled out, "You'll be back!" June thought, "I'm never going back to you." She drove herself and her kids across town to safety and started a new life.

---

25. Johns, *Re-Enchanting the Text*, 144.
26. As Elxa Dal says to Kvothe, "All the truth in the world is held in stories" (Rothfuss, *Wise Man's Fear*, 349).

That story has risen in my family to the role of myth, a meaning-making story. You see, the baby in the story was my mother, Brenda. I heard my grandma tell that story many times, usually because I asked about it. It embodies so many images, symbols, and values in our family: strong women, resiliency, God's active help in times of trouble, love for family, everyone helping out in tough times. Beyond the facts and the details of the story, some of which I know and others I don't, is the gripping narrative of this scared little girl who courageously did what she needed to for her kids. And not insignificant is the reality that the story involves my grandma and my mom, whom I love. And I know the rest of the story, the types of people they became and how the story ends. It's all narrative. It's all story.

To this end, as we progress though the Hero's Journey and the Gospel of Luke, I will be mostly concerned with the story level of the narrative. Other than chapter 1, which serves to set the stage contextually (the mundane world) and prepare us to read Luke's Gospel well, I try not to linger on historical points that distract us from the story. There are myriad commentaries that offer this historical-critical lens; indeed I reference many of them in the footnotes, and if you want to know more of the historical scholarship, I invite you to follow along there. But we want to let the story take center stage. It does for Luke; let it be so for us.

THE CHRIST, CAMPBELL, AND DR. LUKE

As may already be clear, I am a lover of stories. I am also a follower of Jesus. Indeed, we have a number of long-form stories about Jesus in our Christian tradition: the four canonical Gospels. Thus, I felt that it was a worthwhile effort to investigate whether the elements present in Campbell's analysis are also present in the stories of Christ presented two thousand years before. If, in fact, the stories we tell say something about us as humans, then should the story of Christ, the ultimate human, God coming to earth, align in some way with this epic pattern? Or are there major ways that the story of Christ diverges meaningfully from Campbell's pattern? Either way, it seemed to me worth an exploration.[27]

This exploration gives us an opportunity to highlight the epic nature of the story of Christ. Christ is the hero of the story of the New Testament. While this point is hardly novel or controversial, I feel that we sometimes

---

27. Although quite different than this work, Gilbert Bilezikian did an interesting study comparing the Gospel of Mark to a Greek tragedy (*Liberated Gospel*).

Introduction

miss the forest for the trees. That is, we examine individual stories about the parables, miracles, and the life of Christ but sometimes miss the larger, dramatic turns of the narrative.

This is particularly true in Luke-Acts. Luke is telling a long-form narrative in two volumes, the longest corpus of writing in the New Testament.[28] My doctoral work looked at the formation of social identity in Luke-Acts, through the use of stories, cultural memory, and rhetoric. This work helped me see the big picture of Luke-Acts, even while I went deep into specific scenes. It is this approach—keeping the big picture in mind while closely examining key scenes—that will help us see elements of the Hero's Journey in Luke.

So why focus on Luke? The most honest answer is that it is the Gospel I know best and have worked the most with. But additionally, Luke has an intentional narrative structure that lends itself to Jesus being presented as the hero. (I invite Matthean, Markan, and Johannine scholars to engage with Campbell and myself regarding those Gospels and Campbell's work.) I hope this book will introduce the reader of Luke's Gospel to a new quality of the book, that being that Christ is presented in a way that corresponds to so many other hero stories throughout the world and throughout time. Our stories tell us something about us as humans. They also might tell us something about our God who created us.

Let me give you an example. Campbell points out that the two oldest and most dominant story themes are mortality and social order.[29] In other words, our time on this earth in our current existence as humans is fragile and limited; humans would do well to recognize their frailty and their mortality. And second, how we relate to one another is central to our value system. What of my neighbor, my brother, my sister, my enemy?

The story of Jesus answers each of these, clearly and compellingly. The lawyer comes to Jesus in Luke 10:25–37 asking him what he must do to inherit *eternal life*. His is the question of mortality: How does one live beyond this life? How does one make this life matter and continue on to the next? Jesus—in a common moment of gifted pedagogy—puts the question back to the lawyer: "What does the law of Moses say? How do you read it?" The lawyer responds brilliantly, suggesting that one should "love the Lord your God with all your heart, all your soul, all your strength, and all

---

28. Luke-Acts, a two-volume work written by the same author, is longer than all thirteen of the Pauline epistles combined.

29. Campbell, *Myths to Live By*, 22–23.

your mind. And love your neighbor as yourself." "Right!" Jesus told him. "Do this and you will live!" (Luke 10:26–28). In other words, the lawyer rightly determined the key to an abundant and eternal life, to overcoming our limited mortality as humans. And notice that the answer is, remarkably, intimately connected to the social order, loving God and people. In this brief exchange, the student of Jesus has the dominant themes of the history of human storytelling laid plain for them. How do I rise above this mortal existence? Love God and love people. How should I treat my fellow human? Love God and love people. That is it. That is the not-so-secret key to this life.

But if one struggles to apply that, like the lawyer did, Jesus gives more. The lawyer wants to justify himself—don't we all?—and, presumably, not love or be responsible to his neighbor. He wants to know who the exception is. Jesus tells what will become one of his most famous and beloved parables in the church, the parable of the good Samaritan, a story that brilliantly operates on multiple levels. To clarify the most fundamental and ancient questions humans ask, Jesus tells a story.

THE NUCLEAR UNIT OF THE MONOMYTH IN LUKE

In this book I want to take you on a Hero's Journey through the Gospel of Luke. And yet, I am not saying that the story of Jesus follows Campbell's model perfectly. I hope to not overly strain either the story of Jesus or Campbell's model in looking for connections. However, I do hope that as we read and study Luke's story of Jesus, we notice new connections, epic in the way they relate to fundamental human questions that have been asked and answered as long there have been people to ask and answer them. As a confessional scholar, I happen to believe that Jesus is the Messiah, the Son of God, and that his coming to earth was the most significant event in human history. As such, it does not surprise me when we see elements and plot turns in the story of Christ that connect to a larger motif common to many stories told throughout time.

This book is organized around three overarching story divisions that Campbell sees as fundamental to the Hero's Journey: departure, initiation, and return.[30] This is sometimes called the *nuclear unit* or the *monomyth*, the most basic outline of the Hero's Journey. The rest of the points grow from these categories. Campbell, in describing this nuclear unit of the

---

30. Campbell sometimes uses the word "separation" rather than "departure."

Introduction

monomyth, says, "A hero ventures forth from the world of common day into a region of supernatural wonder: fabulous forces are there encountered and a decisive victory is won: the hero comes back from this mysterious adventure with the power to bestow boons on his fellow man."[31]

Part 1 is all about *Departure*. In chapter 1 we examine the setting into which our hero, Jesus is born—which Campbell calls the ordinary or mundane world. This is important because the story—particularly one about a historical place and historical people, like the people of Israel—never starts on the first page, but the prehistory, the context is so important. We can't appreciate the impact that Neo will have in the Matrix until we know something about the war the surviving humans have been in with the machines. Chapter 2 is about the call to adventure; how do the birth narratives set up the story Luke has to tell? Chapter 3 is about the hero receiving supernatural aid, common in hero stories; for Jesus, this is his baptism. Chapter 4—the final chapter of part 1—is about crossing the threshold, Jesus's transition from a private existence to a public ministry.

Part 2 is about *Initiation*, the trials and quests the hero endures on their journey. Jesus certainly encountered his share of trials. Chapter 5 looks at his companions, the disciples, the women, and the other characters in this story. Chapter 6 is about Jesus's road of trials, the Galilean ministry, and the epiphany that happens at the climax of that section, all working to show Jesus as the true Son of God and prophet. Chapter 7 is the journey to Jerusalem, a key organizing feature of Luke's Gospel, building tension as he nears the city. In chapter 8 we look at Jesus's approach, his entry into Jerusalem and his final week. Chapter 9, "The Ordeal," is all about Jesus's arrest and crucifixion, the final battle, as it were.

Part 3—*Return*—is the conclusion of our story. Chapter 10 is all about the resurrection and the encounters Jesus has after the resurrection—key elements for Luke as they set up the sequel, the book of Acts.[32] Finally, I offer a concluding chapter with some encouragement and some closing thoughts on how these ideas can affect an individual or a community.

---

31. Campbell, *Hero with a Thousand Faces*, 30. We may see this threefold pattern at smaller moments in the life of Jesus too. For example, after his baptism, Jesus is sent into the wilderness (departure) to be tempted by Satan (initiation) and returns to Galilee in the power of the Spirit (return). You will begin to notice this nuclear unit of the Hero's Journey in various places in life. But we can also notice it on a larger scale.

32. That is, volume 2, the Acts of the Apostles, which has its own version of the Hero's Journey.

Will you join me as we leave the safety of the world we know, the comfort of the mundane, and journey into the harsh and turbulent story quest of the hero?

DISCUSSION QUESTIONS

1. What are the stories—movies, novels, etc.—that came to mind when thinking about the Hero's Journey?
2. Is there a story that serves those four elements of mythology in your life: inspiring awe, interpreting the cosmos, teaching morality, and helping you endure through crises?
3. Have you ever read the Bible on a story level like you would a short story or a novel? What do you think the benefits of that are/would be?

PART 1

Departure

Only birth can conquer death—the birth, not of the old thing again, but of something new. Within the soul, within the body social, there must be—if we are to experience long survival—a continuous "recurrence of birth" . . . to nullify the unremitting recurrences of death.
—Joseph Campbell, *The Hero with a Thousand Faces*, 16

1

The Mundane World

We have not even to risk the adventure alone; for the heroes of all time have gone before us; the labyrinth is thoroughly known; we have only to follow the thread of the hero-path.

—Joseph Campbell, *The Hero with a Thousand Faces*, 25

So many others have tried their hand at putting together a story of the wonderful harvest of Scripture and history that took place among us, using reports handed down by the original eyewitnesses who served this Word with their very lives. Since I have investigated all the reports in close detail, starting from the story's beginning, I decided to write it all out for you, most honorable Theophilus, so you can know beyond the shadow of a doubt the reliability of what you were taught.

—Luke 1:1–4 MSG

EVERY STORY NEEDS A context, and every hero needs a world to inhabit. Indeed, the first chapter of every new hero story creates a world for the hero to enter—Gotham City for Batman, the Smallville farm and Metropolis for Superman. Campbell calls this the mundane, or ordinary, world; it

Part 1: Departure

is mundane precisely because our hero has not yet come to change it. For Luke's hero story, the setting begins in Judea, extends to Galilee, and by volume 2, ultimately extends much further into the vast expanse of Roman Empire and to the ends of the earth. And since this story is set in a time and place different than our own, we need to make sure we are familiar with the historical and cultural world of our narrative, as the original audience was. When you watch a historical movie, there is often a paragraph of text that precedes the opening scene, setting the historical stage for what is about to come. Or consider the famous "opening crawl" of the original *Star Wars*. Lucas was dropping the viewer into an alien world, into a story already in process, and he needed to establish the normal world for the viewer. Likewise, in order to fully appreciate Luke's hero tale, we must set the stage as well.

Our story starts in Judea in the time of Herod. These details are important, insofar as they enrich and add to the story, rather than distract us from what is happening. These details introduce us to the two primary ways we learn about the setting when we come to Luke. First, we learn about the story's setting through what the author tells us. These are the most important, because the author has brought them specifically to the mind of the reader. These can be overt and front of mind ("In the time of Herod, king of Judah" [Luke 1:3]), or they can be more subversive and merely hinted at ("no prophet is accepted in his hometown" [4:24]).[1] Either way, they are specific mental cues that the author gives the original readers to help them locate the story in time and place.

A second way we find out about the ordinary world in which Luke's hero story takes place is through historical study. Historical study can help us fill in the gaps in order to know more about the time and place our hero lived. This is not required by an original audience, who shares a world with the author. Instead, it is the burden of later readers who come to a text in a different time and place than their own. There are a couple cautions, however, that must be kept in mind as we attempt to fill in these historical gaps.

First, Campbell himself warns against the tendency to reduce all mythological stories to cold history. When we do this, the stories, the symbols, lose their power. "The stressing of this historical element," Campbell

---

1. This is in reference to a larger literary motif in Luke-Acts where Jesus embodies the role of the prophet, which includes rejection from the people as part of that archetype. While I believe that case is made decisively by Luke, it is often done through hints, like this, that require the astute reader to assimilate characteristics from the prophets in the Hebrew Bible. This literary motif will be fleshed out further in ch. 4.

The Mundane World

says, "will lead to confusion; it will simply obfuscate the picture message."[2] As mentioned in the introduction, it is not that we must read the story of Jesus as ahistorical but that the function of the mind that makes meaning dwells at a different level, a higher level with regard to engaging with those symbols. To read mere history is to read a flat, two-dimensional story, and it strips the narrative of its transcendent power. Instead, we want to read the story as story, with an awareness of the historical and cultural contexts. The meaning comes from the story; the context helps frame the story, providing guardrails against our own cultural insertions.

Second, given the limited data available to us, biblical scholars are regularly cautious about equating the world projected by the text and the historical situation we understand about that time period. This caution is apt. At the same time, while the world projected by a text should not be considered a "carbon copy or mirror of the world," it is important for us to acknowledge that the text is at least "anchored in the world."[3] This anchorship relationship between the projected world of the text and the historical realities gives us some permission—though remaining aware of scholarly limitations—to consider historical questions in the reading of Luke's story about Jesus.

However, there is an additional reason specific to Luke that makes utilizing the history of the first century particularly important, namely, that Luke sets his story squarely within the politics and history of the day. Compared to the other canonical Gospels, Luke is most interested in historical events and figures, such as Caesar Augustus (Luke 2:1), Tiberius Caesar (3:1), Caiaphas (3:2), the Herodic dynasty,[4] and more. In addition, Luke likes to describe historically significant locations in his narrative, such as the Jerusalem temple,[5] and into Acts, the Areopagus in Athens (Acts 17) and the temple of Artemis (19:27–37). As Fitzmyer points out, this setting of the coming of the Messiah within a historical perspective seems intentional, not least because Paul seems to suggest it.[6] In Acts 26:26, while telling of his conversion before Festus, Paul states, "The king is familiar

---

2. Campbell, *Hero with a Thousand Faces*, 231.

3. Lundin et al., *Promise of Hermeneutics*, 79. I have a fuller discussion of these elements in Fox, *Hermeneutics of Social Identity*, 7, 19.

4. Luke 1:5; 3:1, 19–20; 8:3; 9:7–9; 13:31; 22:66; 23:7–15; Acts 12:1–23; 13:1; 23:35.

5. Luke 1:9, 21–22; 2:22–37, 41–46; 4:9; 18:10; 19:45–47; 20:1; 21:1–5, 37–38; 22:4, 52–53; 23:45, 53.

6. Fitzmyer, *Luke I–IX*, 172.

PART 1: DEPARTURE

with these things, and I can speak freely to him. I am convinced that none of this has escaped his notice, because it was not done in a corner." Paul is suggesting that the story was significant enough that kings and rulers can be expected to take notice. Indeed, unique from the other Gospel writers, Luke relates the coming of Christ "to persons, times, institutions, and epochs of world history."[7] Thus, to miss the historical flavor, the rich locations, and the politics of Luke's text is to miss an important element of his story. With that in mind, in order to fully equip us to experience the story the way the author intends, the rest of this chapter serves as a historical primer to help us read Luke well.

THE WORLD JESUS ENTERS

The goal of the rest of this chapter is to provide a brief introduction to the world in which Jesus enters so that the reader can make sense of the historical and political situation projected by Luke's narrative. This mundane world can be divided into three categories: the Jewish world, the Roman world, and the enchanted world.

The Jewish World

Luke sets his narrative squarely within the Jewish world. While we rightly note the more universalistic features of Luke's two-volume narrative, namely, the inclusion of God-fearers and gentiles in the work of God, it nonetheless starts as a Jewish story and continues to include Jewish people throughout. The readers find themselves encountering things like the Jewish Levitical priesthood and the duties that go along with that. God's inbreaking into this world will be within the trappings of the Jewish religious system, from the first chapter in Luke to Paul preaching to the Jewish leadership in Acts 28. But an important element to be considered with regard to the Judaism of the first century is the recent history of the Jewish people before the events of Luke-Acts take place.

The period known as the intertestamental period, sometimes called "the silent years,"[8] the few hundred years between when Israel returned

---

7. Fitzmyer, *Luke I–IX*, 172.

8. A professor of mine, Dr. Wave Nunnally, hated this term because although canonical Scripture was not produced during this time (i.e., where the phrase comes from; this is also debatable based on how one dates the postexilic prophets), so much important

from exile in Babylon and the time of the prophets closed, until the stories that make up the Gospels begin, was an extremely contentious period in Israel's history and one that students do well to learn more about. While I offer only a summary here, suggestions for further reading will be made.

Hellenism

The time between the Testaments was a time of growing Hellenism. Hellenism is the rising of Greek culture—language, pluralistic religion, and related practices—as the dominant cultural expression in the centuries leading up to the time of Christ and afterwards. After Alexander the Great conquered areas far and wide—much of what would become the Roman Empire—his death prompted a power struggle among his generals that led to war. The primary conflict that affected Israel was between the Ptolemies and the Seleucids, each having a period of dominance. The Jewish people in Palestine found themselves suffering under the ruling of these dynasties. The earlier period under the Ptolemies was not great and involved occupation, obsessive taxation, and increased Hellenistic influence.[9] However, the time of Seleucid domination was much worse. Antiochus IV Epiphanes launched "an unprecedented anti-Jewish campaign,"[10] required pagan sacrifices, sought to be worshipped, and defiled the temple in Jerusalem.[11] This led to a revolt and the events that occur in the books of 1–2 Maccabees.

After this time of intense persecution, when the very notion of the survival of the Jewish people and the Jewish way of life was threatened, different Jewish groups responded in different ways. Indeed, we ought not to talk of *the Judaism* of the first century of the ancient world but rather *the different Judaisms* that emerged. That is to say, Judaism was (and is) very diverse. We encounter a number of groups in Luke that represent responses to this crisis.[12]

---

stuff was going on and God was still engaging with his people. As a result I still cringe a little at this term because of his great influence.

9. For a much fuller description and history of the Ptolemaic period, see Athas, *Bridging the Testaments*, 195–263.

10. Helyer, "Hasmoneans," 39.

11. Burge and Green, *New Testament in Antiquity*, 29–66. See also Athas, *Bridging the Testaments*, 270–306.

12. For a helpful and accessible guide to this region is K. C. Hanson and Oakman, *Palestine*.

Part 1: Departure

Pharisees

Perhaps the most recognized group for the modern reader is the Pharisees.[13] The Pharisees are Jews who, in response to persecution that nearly wiped them out, doubled down on holiness, that is, a strict observance of the law. Indeed, Pharisees sought to follow the law as closely and as carefully as possible.[14]

However, the unfortunate by-product of this intensified holiness is that the Pharisees disregard and implicate those they perceive as "sinners," putting them on a trajectory to clash with Jesus. Luke-Acts is kinder to the Pharisees than are the other Gospels. While Matthew, Mark, and John envision the Pharisees as a lethal threat to Jesus, Luke presents them as mostly righteous with regard to their religious practice but does critique them specifically with regard to their hypocrisy and exclusion of outsiders.[15] In the vast majority of these encounters, the Pharisees are objecting to Jesus for some ritual offense, such as healing on the Sabbath or associating with sinners and tax collectors. Given what we know about their intensity for the law and that Jesus was concerned with engaging the poor and outcasts, these conflicts between Jesus and the Pharisees make sense. However, a few encounters in Luke are worthy of special mention.

Twice the narrator (as opposed to characters in the story) comments on the Pharisees, the first in 7:30, suggesting since the Pharisees had not been baptized by John, they "rejected God's purposes for themselves." This is a bold statement of critique against the Pharisees and their rejection of what God is doing. The second place the narrator speaks about the Pharisees is in 16:14 where the text states that they loved money. In addition to the narrator, Jesus, too, is critical of the Pharisees. They are the sole target of the first two of Jesus's woes in 11:42–43. He also warns his disciples against their hypocrisy (12:1) and tells a parable against them (18:9–14). However, despite this overwhelming timbre of conflict and critique, not all

---

13. See Sievers and Levine, *Pharisees*, which is an important recent volume that goes into significant depth regarding this conspicuous group in the Gospels. See also Bock and Komoszewski, *Jesus*.

14. Josephus states, "On account of which doctrines they are able greatly to persuade the body of the people: and whatsoever they do about divine worship, prayers, and sacrifices, they perform them according to their direction. Insomuch, that the cities give great attestations to them, on account of their entire virtuous conduct, both in the actions of their lives, and their discourses also" (*Ant.* 18.1.3 §15).

15. Mason has a good summary of the views of the different Gospels ("Josephus's Pharisees," 110).

of the content about the Pharisees is negative in Luke. For example, many of these conflicts come out of Pharisees offering hospitality to Jesus in their homes,[16] and several of these come after bold statements the Pharisees make considering "what they might do to Jesus" (6:11) or that they "oppose him fiercely" (11:53). They still warn him (13:31) that Herod is trying to kill him.

Thus, it appears that Luke has included the most significant encounters with the Pharisees that highlight Jesus's mission to the poor and the outcasts, which necessarily involves conflict and critique. Pharisees are notably absent from the conspiracy around Jesus's death, while the main character of the book of Acts, Paul, will maintain his Pharisaic identity in his ministry (Acts 23:6). Thus, despite these conflicts, when compared to the other Jewish groups of the time, Jesus is arguably most like the Pharisees, and his ongoing engagement with them seems to suggest that they chose to be around him, even when their philosophies differed and despite Jesus's prophetic critique of them.[17]

Other Jewish Groups

There are other Jewish groups in addition to Pharisees that are important to be aware of in the mundane world of the first-century landscape. Sadducees are the wealthy Jewish aristocracy of the first century. We also know that they denied elements like the bodily resurrection, angels, and the like, things that are common in Luke's enchanted world.[18] Sadducees are mentioned only one time in Luke, when they engage Jesus regarding marriage after the resurrection (20:27–40). Given what we know about the Sadducees, we see that their question of Jesus in Jerusalem appears to be in bad faith.[19] Sadducees are present in Acts serving on the Sanhedrin (4:1; 5:17) and in Paul's trial (Acts 23), arguing with the Pharisees about the resurrection.

Essenes make up the group of desert separatists who have chosen to remove themselves from society, the temple, and the other elements of mainstream religion and culture, instead living in communities in the desert. However, Essenes also might have existed in smaller communities

---

16. Luke 7:36–50; 11:37–41; 14:1–24.
17. More will be said on Jesus's role of the prophet in ch. 4.
18. For more on the Sadducees, see Strauss, "Sadducees."
19. Lee-Barnewall, "Pharisees, Sadducees, and Essenes," 221.

"throughout cities and villages" in Judea.[20] We do not encounter Essenes directly in the New Testament, although certain scholars wonder about certain characters' connection with them and their influence over elements of Judaism in the first century. Likewise, while they do not occur directly in Luke, their understanding of the corruption of the temple and the chief priests gives us an idea of the range of views in the first century.

Jewish Revolts and Revolutionary Movements

There were also various Jewish revolts and different kinds of revolutionary groups in the first century. Josephus mentions several different groups that can be understood as revolutionaries, including the Zealots, the Sicarii, and a group he calls "the Fourth Philosophy" (with Pharisees, Sadducees, and Essenes making up the first three). Exactly how these groups relate to one another—or if the Fourth Philosophy refers to one or all of these groups—is unclear and a matter of scholarly debate.[21] However, it is clear that there were pockets of resistance to both Rome and the Jewish aristocracy that were willing to use violence to assert their influence.

Luke and Acts each mentions one of the disciples of Jesus as Simon the Zealot (Luke 6:15; Acts 1:13), although some scholars doubt whether that is a reference to the political movement.[22] While zealots do not play an important role in Luke-Acts, their ideology shows us another example of the range of responses that different Jewish groups had to the turmoil and existential threat the intertestamental period posed to the Jewish people.

While much more could be said about the Jewish world into which Jesus enters, I will save more pertinent discussions for when they come up in the text.

The Roman World

The reader must not forget that the events of Luke-Acts take place in Roman captivity. In an age of empires ruling large swaths of land with numerous

---

20. Lee-Barnewall, "Pharisees, Sadducees, and Essenes," 221.

21. *Ant.* 18.1.6 §§23–25. See Heard and Yamazaki-Ransom, "Revolutionary Movements"; Horsley, *Bandits, Prophets, and Messiahs*.

22. Heard and Yamazaki-Ransom argue that the zealots were not officially formed until the 60s, so that must be more of a characterizing name ("Revolutionary Movements," 796).

The Mundane World

diverse people groups under their purview—the Roman Empire embodying this reality most clearly—it made for an oftentimes tense and oppressive dynamic for those on the underside of power.

Rome had their own mythological origin story that filled the leaders and citizens with imperialistic pride and transcendent pathos. The twin brothers Romulus and Remus were fathered by Mars, the god of war. King Amulius saw them as possible threats for the throne and ordered them abandoned and killed. The river god, Tiberinus, saved them and delivered them to a mother wolf who nursed and raised them in the wild, along with a local shepherd. As they aged, their natural leadership qualities showed themselves, and they drew a following from many people. They desired to build a city on a certain region with seven hills, but in a disagreement over which hill to build it on, Romulus killed Remus and ruled the new city named after him (i.e., Rome) as its first king.[23]

Like all myths, this one, too, has symbols and values vested in the elements of the story. What are the values you notice from that myth? Intervention from the gods to bring forth Rome. Natural leadership. The gritty, harsh conditions of being raised by wolves. War (i.e., the war god) and fratricide. The seven hills of Rome. Indeed, all of these (and more) are apt descriptors of the Roman ethos, a nation that ruled with legions of soldiers, conquered foreign lands, and sought to maintain peace and order in the vast lands they ruled, by force if necessary.

This period of relative prosperity while trying to maintain internal peace is called the Pax Romana, and it lasted from the rise of Caesar Augustus in 27 BCE until the death of Marcus Aurelius in 180 CE. During this period, two elements are central and crucially important to the Romans as they rule their vast and diverse lands.

1. Taxes

The people must pay their taxes. This is how the empire funds their conquests and the lavish lives of the leaders (i.e., Caesar, Herod, Pilate, etc.). The result is prolonged financial insecurity for many or most of those underneath the rule of that empire. Scholars estimate that nearly 70 percent lived at or below subsistence level.[24] These subjects, in exchange for their taxes,

---

23. Dionysius of Halicarnassus, *Roman Antiquities*, vol. 1, chs. 71–87. See also Livy, *Early History*, 33–37.

24. Downs, "Economics, Taxes, and Tithes," 159.

PART 1: DEPARTURE

are for the most part left alone. Scholars differ as to how they understand the burden of taxes, recognizing that this likely ebbed and flowed with time. Despite the assumption of the hefty financial burden that taxation put on the Jewish people, there are hints that they experience a time of modest but relative wealth.[25] We see a situation in Luke where communities of people are traveling yearly from Galilee to Jerusalem for the Passover Festival (Luke 2:41).[26] This is possible only in times of relative wealth but is more possible when communities of people band together for mutual support and the sharing of burdens.

Luke offers an interesting commentary on taxation in his Gospel. This happens primarily through the exploration of characters who are tax collectors, that is, Jews working for the Romans to collect taxes from their fellow Jews and getting wealthy in the process.[27] This earns them a position of being exceptionally disliked by other Jews, in that they are regularly grouped in with prostitutes and "sinners."[28] They play an important role in Luke's narrative, not only in that one of Jesus's disciples, Levi, is a tax collector but also in a second character who seeks out Jesus, named Zacchaeus, and that numerous unnamed tax collectors are often around Jesus.[29] These characters serve as foils for the Pharisees, who continually struggle with Jesus's association with whom they deem as unworthy and particularly sinful people. However, it is also interesting to note that one of the charges Jesus's accusers will bring against him to the Romans is his failure to pay taxes to Rome (Luke 23:2).

2. Keep the Peace

Rome knew the difficulty of leading vast lands made up of numerous different ethnic groups, with their various religions and cultures, and the ever-present potential for riotous ways. The empire vows to keep the peace in their land through military presence and authority. This begins at the top, with Caesar, flowing down to the kings and vassals, to the leaders of the soldiers and the soldiers themselves, who play a sort of policing role in

---

25. Downs, "Economics, Taxes, and Tithes," 164.

26. It may be that the communities travel for the other pilgrimage festivals, too, although Luke records only this one.

27. Athas, *Bridging the Testaments*, 233–34.

28. Luke 5:30–32; 6:32–34; 7:34, 37–39; 15:1; 19:7.

29. Luke 5:30; 7:34; 15:1.

Palestine in the time of Jesus. A particular fear of the Romans during this time was political unrest, or riots. The reason Jesus is a perceived threat to Rome is his ability to draw crowds of thousands in Jerusalem during the Passover Festival. As Luke 19:47–48 states, "Every day he was teaching at the temple. But the chief priests, the teachers of the law and the leaders among the people were trying to kill him. Yet they could not find any way to do it, because all the people hung on his words."

Luke is also going to tell us of significant encounters Jesus has with Romans. Beyond his trial before Pilate and Herod, both leaders of Roman jurisdictions, Luke features Roman soldiers in his narrative. While this will be more significant in Acts (namely Cornelius but also Sergius Paulus), Jesus has a significant encounter with a centurion in Luke 7:1–10. There are numerous elements in this encounter that give us a window into the mundane world of first-century Palestine. Two obvious and often-cited elements are that Jesus heals the servant of a gentile Roman centurion and that the centurion displays great faith and trust in Jesus, which Jesus comments on ("I tell you, I have not found such great faith even in Israel" [7:9]). But beyond those significant elements, we also see an interesting communal element of Capernaum. The Jewish elders in the town go to Jesus to ask for help for the centurion and plead with him earnestly, "This man deserves to have you do this, because he loves our nation and has built our synagogue" (Luke 7:4b–5). Despite the very real elements of Roman oppression—ruling over Jewish lands, taxation, even crucifixion—some communities reflected relative harmony between the local Roman authorities and the Jewish leadership in the town. This apparently went both ways, as the centurion built the Jews a synagogue. We must imagine that Roman authorities helping Jewish people build a place of worship in the town as something of an outlier in this era; however, it is not altogether surprising.

The positive encounter with the centurion is going to stand in contrast to most of Jesus's interactions with Roman leadership in Luke. Luke makes it clear that Herod is evil when John rebukes Herod for marrying his brother's wife "and all the other evil things he had done" (3:19). On top of those things, Herod throws John in prison. Luke does not tell the story of John's execution as in Matthew and Mark. In Luke 13:31, the Pharisees warn Jesus that Herod is trying to kill him. Jesus responds by calling him a fox. This was a pejorative term, one accusing Herod of destructiveness and bad character.[30] Jesus restates his commitment to journey to Jerusalem for his

---

30. Parsons, *Luke*, 225. Parsons suggests that those elements of critique continue in the next verse, which challenges Jerusalem.

death. However, in the midst of these contentious sections between Herod and Jesus, Luke also tells us of Joanna, the wife of Chuza: the husband is the manager (ἐπιτρόπου) of Herod; the wife a follower of and supporter of Jesus.

Indeed, it appears the reality of Roman rule provides significant content for Luke's Gospel. While Luke does not undermine the harsh reality that Roman occupation brings to this part of the world, he is careful to show how God's work includes Roman gentiles. We encounter Herod again along with Pilate at the trial of Jesus, which we will discuss in chapter 9, "The Ordeal."

Before we end our discussion of the Roman world into which our hero is born, we must talk about a particular benefit of Roman prosperity during the time of the Pax Romana. This was a time of relative stability for this part of the world. Coming out of the turbulent centuries before, having one empire in charge, even a harsher one like Rome, allowed for Jesus's mission to go forward. That sentence may sound crazy with realities like crucifixion, the destruction of Jerusalem, and the persecution the early Christians face. However legitimately terrible those elements are, Roman rule is an improvement over what came before. Stability brought about roads for easier travel and a common language, Koine Greek, which made the spreading of the gospel—and the writings of the New Testament—much easier.

Enchantment

Perhaps the most important element of the mundane world Luke introduces his readers to is that it is enchanted. By enchanted, I mean that miraculous and spiritual things are beginning to happen; God is at work.[31] The enchantment present in Luke is specifically related to the coming of Christ. Angels foretell his birth. Old saints prophesy concerning our hero. There are dark forces, too, as demons manifest in Jesus's presence, recognizing him as the Holy One of God, and the devil himself tries to make Jesus stumble. Jesus works miracles and casts out demons, and he will empower others to do the same. Even after he ascends, his followers will perform miracles and other heroic acts as his enduring Spirit enables them. But this element of enchantment is crucially important for the coming of our hero. It creates the conditions by which God is able to break into the mundane

---

31. Taylor suggests that enchantment's antonym, disenchantment, is a key feature of our modern secular society and has helped the rise of atheism (*Secular Age*, 25–28).

The Mundane World

world. He has not forgotten his faithful people, nor will he neglect to cross expansive valleys to call back those who are far from him.

This is true for Zechariah and Elizabeth, and it is where our story starts. They are a righteous, priestly couple who have remained faithful in a dark time in Israel's history. They are in their old age and do not have a child. They have been inflicted with barrenness and infertility. The grief and deferred longing must be crushing to them. And yet, they remain faithful. Zechariah practices his priestly rituals, wondering if God will break in to his mundane world.

At the same time, what is happening with Zechariah and Elizabeth is happening in a bigger way with Israel. As Israel labors under the oppression of Rome, many persist in their faithfulness, longing for the consolation of Israel (Isa 40). As Zechariah hopes for a son, Israel hopes for a Messiah. Will God break into their mundane world, they wonder.

Perhaps there is even a third level, beyond even that of Zechariah and Elizabeth, and contextually with Israel, to the universal level of all of humanity. We will see that Luke, like Isaiah, has a universal scope to his adventure. The priestly couple represent not only Israel, but they are stand-ins for all of humanity who long for something more. It could be a baby, or a new job, or healing. Maybe it is justice or forgiveness. We all can relate to being in the cold and cruel mundane world hoping for something to happen to break us out of this current struggle, this current prison of silence, hoping for breakthrough, hoping for our moment of spiritual passage.

And then we notice ripples on the surface of life.

DISCUSSION QUESTIONS

1. Which of the background elements discussed do you see as the most significant?
2. Would you call our world enchanted? How have you seen God break into the world?
3. How can you relate to the longing of Zechariah and Elizabeth, Israel, and all of humanity in your own life and experience?

2

The Call to Adventure

The hero as the incarnation of God is himself the navel of the world, the umbilical point through which the energies of eternity break into time. Thus the world navel is the symbol of the continuous creation: the mystery of the maintenance of the world through that continuous miracle of vivification which wells within all things.
—Joseph Campbell, *The Hero with a Thousand Faces*, 41

In the sixth month of Elizabeth's pregnancy, God sent the angel Gabriel to the Galilean village of Nazareth to a virgin engaged to be married to a man descended from David. His name was Joseph, and the virgin's name, Mary. Upon entering, Gabriel greeted her:

Good morning!
You're beautiful with God's beauty,
Beautiful inside and out!
God be with you.

She was thoroughly shaken, wondering what was behind a greeting like that. But the angel assured her, "Mary, you have nothing to fear. God has a surprise for you: You will become pregnant and give birth to a son and call his name Jesus."

—Luke 1:26–31 MSG

The Call to Adventure

AFTER NEO FALLS ASLEEP at his computer, the computer begins to do weird things. It wakes him up. It tells him the Matrix has him. It tells him to follow the white rabbit. Just then, there is a knock at the door—also predicted by the computer—and one of those at the door has a tattoo of a white rabbit. The people invite him to come with them, and alas, Neo's adventure begins.

Hero tales often have a scene where the hero is called to adventure. Moses encounters the burning bush. Luke Skywalker sees the message from Princess Leia stored in R2D2. Having established the mundane world the hero is a part of, the story thrusts the hero into the adventure. Likewise in Luke, there must be a beginning to this adventure. We noted at the end of last chapter that ripples were stirring on the surface of Luke's enchanted world. This world is ready for a hero to enter. But in order for that to happen, there must be a call.

The call to adventure is no small matter. Every hero must hear the call. This story is about the Messiah, God come to earth, and it requires a company of co-conspirators to help set the stage for our hero. To brace for his arrival, we encounter three separate calls to adventure, humans who have a front-row seat to the coming of the hero and who participate in his advent. In Campbell's model, the call to adventure is the call to the hero; in this sense, Luke's Gospel does not fit hand in glove with that call. Rather, I am choosing to focus on how the author strategically brings other characters into the story—their own calls to adventure to help welcome the hero.

ZECHARIAH AND ELIZABETH

The first characters in our story are an old priestly couple, Zechariah and Elizabeth. The characters are iconic; they play an important part early in the Gospel, and we see the genius of Luke, the storyteller from the first chapter. A few features to notice.

First, Luke features many characters in his narrative. Some will occur for a scene or two, serve their purpose, and then disappear from the narrative as the story moves on to other things. You can think of the focus of the narrative like a camera that is filming a movie; sometimes the camera of the narrative moves on to other characters. Zechariah and Elizabeth are an excellent example of this. They play an important role early and then depart the scene. Elizabeth is not mentioned after chapter 1, and Zechariah is mentioned only in connection with being John's father. However, they are

Part 1: Departure

the perfect couple to start this hero's tale. This is true of hero stories as well; the narrative camera follows the hero.

A second feature of Luke's storytelling is that Luke is quick to praise certain characters in the narrative. This is a feature called *ethos* borrowed from ancient rhetoric, where building up the reputation and import of the character before they give a speech is as important as the content of the speech.[1] Luke does this with regard to speeches,[2] but he also does it with the characters in his narrative. This happens in two ways, either through the words of the characters in the story, as with the centurion (Luke 7:4–5) and John the Baptist (7:24–28), or directly as the narrator, as with Stephen (Acts 6:8), Cornelius (Acts 10), Apollos (Acts 18:24–26), and here, with Zechariah and Elizabeth.

Third, Luke-Acts is rife with doubling, that is, characters are paired together in the narrative. For example, both Zechariah and Mary receive messages from the same angelic visitor; in response, they each sing a song about their experiences.[3] When Jesus is presented at the temple, two characters are there to speak words over the baby: Simeon and Anna (Luke 2:25–38). In the synagogue at Nazareth, Jesus will refer to the stories of the widow of Zarephath and Naaman the Syrian (4:25–27). Regularly the author will place miracles of Jesus adjacent for comparative purposes, for example, the demon-possessed man in Capernaum and Peter's mother-in-law (4:33–39), the centurion and the widow of Nain (7:1–17), and many others. This continues into Acts with Ananias and Sapphira (5:1–11), the healings of Aeneas and Tabitha (9:32–43), and the conversions and baptisms of Lydia and the jailer, with their respective households (16:1–34).

We are told that not only is Zechariah a practicing priest, but Elizabeth, too, is "from the daughters of Aaron" (1:5). This couple is double-dipped in priestly lineage. More than that, Luke tells us they are both "righteous in the sight of God, observing all of the Lord's commands and decrees blamelessly" (1:6). If one were to think that this mundane world is bereft of faithful, righteous people of God, Luke quells that temptation straightaway. Despite their faithfulness and faithful service as a priestly family, they are "very old" and without a child. They stand in a long line of faithful Hebrew people who have struggled with barrenness—a condition that was oftentimes seen

---

1. See Fox, *Hermeneutics of Social Identity*, 183–231.

2. Consider Stephen's introduction and speech before the Sanhedrin in Acts 6–7 and Paul's conversion in Acts 9, leading up to his first speech in Acts 13.

3. Luke 1:5–23, 26–38, 46–56, 67–79.

The Call to Adventure

as a curse or judgment from God and had significant spiritual overtones.[4] However, Luke has told us of the righteousness and blamelessness of this couple. This is a significant tension the reader should feel; what do we make of a situation where a faithful and righteous priestly couple experiences such a negative spiritual consequence? Surely this calls for the attention and intervention of the living God![5]

In Zechariah and Elizabeth we are meant to recall Abram and Sarai, the old childless couple whom God chooses to start the nation of Israel (Gen 12). From a human perspective, choosing an old childless couple to start a nation is a bad move. But God operates differently. In a strikingly similar way, God is choosing another old childless couple to start something new in Luke.

It is through God's providence that Zechariah is chosen by lot to burn incense in the temple—a once-in-a-lifetime opportunity.[6] While Zechariah is burning incense, an angel appears to him beside the altar—a clear sign of the enchanted world our story inhabits—and tells him his prayer has been heard. Is there anything better to hear from a heavenly messenger than assurance that the thing you have been praying for your whole life has been heard by God and will be answered? It is a call to adventure he certainly will not decline.

Campbell observes that the herald or announcer of adventure throughout many stories is often "dark, loathly, or terrifying, judged evil by the world."[7] By stark contrast, the heralds of adventure in Luke are angels: heavenly, holy, and surrounded by the glory of God, yet no less terrifying than the dark figures of fiction. This difference highlights the enchantment stirring on the surface of the mundane world.

The angel tells of the future ministry of John. Zechariah, despite the positive picture painted of him so far, struggles to believe the words of the heavenly messenger and asks for proof. His doubting may be an example of what Campbell calls the refusal of the call. Fortunately for Zechariah, "not

---

4. Elizabeth herself will call it a "disgrace among the people" (1:25). For a full look at the role of barrenness in the Hebrew Scriptures, see Baden, "Nature of Barrenness."

5. Brown sees connections here with the story of Samuel, the priest: his mother, Hannah, struggled with barrenness and cried out to God; there are similarities in the intro formulae of 1 Sam 1:1 and Luke 1:5, and both Samuel and John are Nazarites (1 Sam 1:11; Luke 1:15) (Brown, *Birth of the Messiah*, 268).

6. Bock, *Luke*, 1:79.

7. Campbell, *Hero with a Thousand Faces*, 53.

all who hesitate are lost."[8] He does, however, lose his voice until the birth of the child. His doubt is balanced by Elizabeth's joy—perhaps the primary emotional tone of the Lukan birth narratives—who says in 1:25, "The Lord has done this for me. . . . In these days he has shown his favor and taken away my disgrace among the people."[9]

The names of many of the characters are significant in Luke. Zechariah (God remembers) has his prayer remembered by God. The meaning of Elizabeth is debated, meaning either "God is my oath" or "God is my fortune"; either one fits the motif of God providing her with a child, who is named John (graced by God), whose story will prove his name is apt. This news is told by Gabriel (God is my strength), who stands in the presence of God and is a fine representative of God's strength to redeem his people.[10]

And with that, the first call to adventure in the form of a birth narrative merges with a second.

MARY

After this, the narrative camera follows the heavenly messenger, Gabriel, who stands in the presence of God and travels north to appear in Nazareth. There he finds a virgin pledged to be married to a man named Joseph, descended from David. We note the important move from the priestly to the kingly, the Levitical to the messianic.

While we learned about Zechariah and Elizabeth through direct dictation from the narrator, we will learn about Mary through what she says and what others say about her. While Gabriel's words to Zechariah focused on God answering his prayer, the words to Mary emphasize her favor: "Greetings, you who are highly favored! The Lord is with you" (1:28). While she is troubled by this, the angel states a second time that she has found favor with God. While Zechariah and Elizabeth were noteworthy because of their righteous obedience, Mary stands out because of her favor with the Almighty.[11]

---

8. Campbell, *Hero with a Thousand Faces*, 64.

9. The theme of joy is mentioned four times in the birth narrative: Luke 1:14, 44, 58; 2:10.

10. For more on the use of names as a rhetorical strategy in Luke-Acts, see Fox, *Hermeneutics of Social Identity*, 93–95.

11. The meaning of Mary's name is less clear; Bock (*Luke*, 1:106) and Fitzmyer (*Luke I–IX*, 343) suggest it means "excellence."

The Call to Adventure

As with John, Gabriel foretells of the baby, who shall be named Jesus (God saves), and his remarkable identity and ministry. Mary, like Zechariah, questions the remarkable news; however, she does not doubt and ask for a sign, rather, just asks for clarity regarding how this might be accomplished.[12] Gabriel explains a bit more about the remarkable nature of the conception and ties this miracle to the pregnancy of Mary's relative, Elizabeth, who is in her sixth month, ending with the perfectly enchanted statement, "For no word from God will ever fail" (1:37). Mary responds in obedience, accepting her call to adventure: "I am the Lord's servant. May your word to me be fulfilled" (1:38).

At this point, the two birth narratives are woven together as these two remarkable women with miraculous pregnancies meet in the hill country of Judea. Upon hearing Mary's greeting, the baby leaps in his mother's womb and Elizabeth is filled with the Holy Spirit—a first occurrence for Luke, which will become a common theme in Acts. We are reminded again (1:45) that, despite any and all evidence to the contrary, the Lord fulfills his promises.

In the next three scenes we see two songs from these early characters, Mary's Magnificat and Zechariah's Benedictus.[13] These songs give the author an opportunity to bathe the narrative in rich imagery that prepares the reader for what is about to follow. With these poetic interludes, much like a musical that uses songs and choreography to advance the plot and heighten the emotion of the production, Luke weaves a tapestry of the old and the new, with Old Testament imagery meeting the new thing God is doing.[14]

In between these scenes is the story of John's birth and naming; Zechariah's speech is returned, allowing him to break forth into his song of praise to God. The scene ends with John growing and becoming strong in spirit in the wilderness. John's own call to adventure, having started with his parents and been prophesied by an angel, is complete. When we see John again it will be as the word of God comes to him in the wilderness.

---

12. Bock, *Luke*, 1:118.

13. These canticles, along with Simeon's below, are traditionally named by the first words of the song in the Latin translation of these texts.

14. For a more thorough breakdown of the imagery and intertextuality in the canticles, see Fox, *Hermeneutics of Social Identity*, 97–117.

Part 1: Departure

THE SHEPHERDS

The next characters called to adventure on this heroic tale are the least likely we have seen yet. Zechariah and Elizabeth are a strange choice as the parents of the forerunner of the Messiah because of their age and childlessness, but their righteousness makes them stand out as exemplary. Mary, too, would be regarded as an unspectacular young girl if it wasn't for her great favor and obedience as God's servant. But the shepherds are different.

The social status of the shepherds has been an issue of scholarly debate. Jeremias, famously, labeled them as "dishonest and thieving"[15] and quotes a later Jewish source, which says, "There was no more disreputable occupation than that of a shepherd."[16] However, more recent scholars have pushed back on that harsh view, instead relegating shepherds to the peasantry, "located toward the bottom of the scale of power and privilege."[17] This is fitting, as while Luke will report on the full swath of social spectrum's response to the good news of Jesus, special attention will be given to the lowly, the minor characters.[18]

The shepherds get their own brush with the enchanted. In words famous to churchgoers as the text read at Christmas, shepherds are watching their flocks at night when an angel appears to them with the glory of God shining in the darkness. Unlike the two previous angelic visitations, we are not told that this is Gabriel. The message that a Savior has been born is delivered:

> Do not be afraid. I bring you good news that will cause great joy for all the people. Today in the town of David a Savior has been born to you; he is the Messiah, the Lord. This will be a sign to you: You will find a baby wrapped in cloths and lying in a manger. (Luke 2:10–12)

---

15. Jeremias, *Jerusalem*, 305.
16. Jeremias, *Jerusalem*, 311n42, quoting Midrash Ps 23:2.
17. Green, *Gospel of Luke*, 130n39. See also Parsons, *Luke*, 53–54.
18. As best I can tell, this term was coined by Rhoads et al., *Mark as Story*, 130–31. While Rhoads et al. speak of minor characters as characters who have a small part to play in the narrative and are oftentimes marginalized figures, I define *minor characters* as "those characters that the reader is surprised play a significant part in the narrative due to certain roadblocks, be they social, racial, gender based, or otherwise" (*Hermeneutics of Social Identity*, 64). My use of the term is not based on how big of a role they play in the narrative but solely on their standing in their parent culture.

The Call to Adventure

The sign that a Savior has been born is that a baby is wrapped in cloths and laying in a manger. A baby wrapped in cloths is not a surprising announcement. One would rightly expect that all of the babies born in Palestine during this period of lower economic standing would be wrapped in cloths—not the fancy purple robes of a king's palace but the humble cloths of the lowly. However, familiarity robs us of the truly shocking nature of a baby being laid in a manger, a feeding trough for animals. Of all the babies born in that region—and perhaps the inhabited world at that time—only one baby is laid in a messy feeding trough. It is so unique that it is the sign the angel gives the shepherds to be able to recognize the child. Immediately the angel is joined by a great company of angels, praising God. The shepherds hurry off on their own adventure, finding the baby as they were told. They spread the word about this remarkable event and become some of the first to spread the good news about this child to the people.

THE ADVENT OF THE HERO

The author challenges us, implicitly, to identify with these characters. The old and righteous but phased out; the humble and unassuming servant; the rough-and-tumble shepherds in the countryside; each of these characters help set the stage for the coming of the hero.

With the birth of our hero, we have two childhood scenes that help flesh out this character before his appearance as an adult in chapter 3. The first is the presentation of Jesus at the temple. The story has brought us to the temple before; indeed it was the setting of our first brush with enchantment as Zechariah encountered the angel. Here again we will see the enchantment of God surrounding the advent of this remarkable child. Campbell notes how the whole hero life, including childhood, is "a pageant of marvels with the great central adventure as its culmination."[19]

Jesus's parents take him to the temple, careful to do what is required in the law of Moses regarding purification and offerings. At the temple we meet Simeon (God has heard). Luke tells us that he is waiting for "the consolation of Israel" (Isa 40); indeed *God has heard* his people and is answering them in the advent of our hero. The narrator describes Simeon as "righteous and devout" and that "the Holy Spirit was on him," having a revelation that he would see the Messiah before he died (Luke 2:26). A moment of great consequence is at hand for both Simeon and the reader.

---

19. Campbell, *Hero with a Thousand Faces*, 319.

Part 1: Departure

Taking him in his arms at that moment, he breaks forth into our third musical number of the story, the Nunc Dimittis. Simeon's song is shorter than the others but similarly foresees the future impact of the ministry of our hero, including both Israel and gentiles in the scope of God's redemptive plan, and is followed by words that give the first hints of the controversial and dangerous nature of Jesus's ministry. No hero walks a path devoid of obstacles. Simeon's dramatic statement in his opening line, "You may now dismiss your servant in peace," is akin to "I can now die happy." The Messiah is the culmination of hopes from time immemorial.

Simeon is paired with a female counterpart, Anna, called a prophet. Again, the narrator tells the reader her ethos: an old widow, connected to the temple day and night, fasting and praying, and in the company of those "looking forward to the redemption of Jerusalem." Establishing her reputation is particularly significant here, as we are not told what she says; rather, we are given a narrative summary that she spoke about the child and his connection to redemption. Simeon and Anna, like Zechariah and Elizabeth before them, represent the patient seekers of God in the mundane world. Again, if one cynically and nihilistically assumes that the world lacks a faithful righteous remnant, Luke is careful to demonstrate otherwise.

A final scene of Jesus's childhood—the only story we have in the canonical Gospels about Jesus as a young person after he was no longer a baby—occurs once again around the Jerusalem temple. This time Jesus's family travels from Nazareth to Jerusalem for the Feast of Passover. The story quickly moves to the conclusion of the festival, where despite the family returning home, Jesus stays in Jerusalem without the knowledge of his parents. All parents can imagine the terror of looking for their child for three days among hundreds of thousands of people present for one of the pilgrimage festivals. But more than this empathetic connection, we see something remarkable about this child: he is in his Father's house (i.e., the temple courts). He is also engaging with the teachers and asking them questions—as he will do in his later ministry—and they are amazed at him. As his birth made perfectly clear, we are now reminded in his adolescence: this is no ordinary child. A remarkable hero requires a remarkable childhood.

However, the story then jumps ahead nearly two decades. Common in hero stories around the world, "the child of destiny has to face a long period of obscurity."[20] The nature of Jesus's childhood is obscure precisely because we know nothing of it, save the one story Luke has told us. His miraculous

---

20. Campbell, *Hero with a Thousand Faces*, 326.

The Call to Adventure

advent in the first two stories prepares us for an equally enchanted adult life.

CONCLUSION

And with this, the call to adventure is complete. While our hero has arrived for the journey, it is the co-conspirators who are called to adventure, called out of their comfort zones to welcome the hero onto the stage. The readers, too, are invited into this adventure, to prepare their ears to hear what the hero will teach us. But before the hero's quest can truly begin, he must obtain something to help him on his journey. We now look at the supernatural aid given to our hero.

DISCUSSION QUESTIONS

1. Which of the characters who is called to adventure do you identify with most?
2. Much of the content of this chapter is associated with Christmas. Do you think the familiarity of the Christmas story to most people leads us to miss the fascination of the story level? If so, how do we get that back?
3. What is your favorite part of the story of birth and childhood of Jesus? Which parts do you see as most significant for his future ministry?

3

Supernatural Aid

A hero ventures forth from the world of common day into a region of supernatural wonder: fabulous forces are there encountered and a decisive victory is won.

—Joseph Campbell, *The Hero with a Thousand Faces*, 30

After all the people were baptized, Jesus was baptized. As he was praying, the sky opened up and the Holy Spirit, like a dove descending, came down on him. And along with the Spirit, a voice: "You are my Son, chosen and marked by my love, pride of my life."

—Luke 3:21–22 MSG

THE OLD MAN, BEN Kenobi, tells young Luke Skywalker: "The Force is what gives a Jedi his power. It's an energy field created by all living things. It surrounds us and penetrates us. It binds the galaxy together."[1] Not long after this, Luke, having found his uncle and aunt killed by imperial troops, returns to Ben and asks him to train him in the ways of the Force. Ben gives him his father's lightsaber and begins to teach him the ways of a Jedi.

1. Lucas, *New Hope*, 34:37.

Supernatural Aid

This classic scene in the iconic movie sets the stage for the most famous space drama to date. Yet, it is rooted in a much older feature of storytelling that Campbell inclines us to: supernatural aid coming to the hero. Supernatural aid comes in all forms: old crones (or old man Ben Kenobi), fairy godmothers, the virgin Mary, and the Holy Ghost.[2] James Bond has the gadgets provided him by Q. Batman has the utility belt. Superman has superpowers inherent in him from his home planet, Krypton. Neo can manipulate the natural laws in the Matrix. For Jesus it is his special connection with the Father and the empowering of the Holy Spirit.

JOHN AND JESUS

In order to deal with Jesus's baptism and the supernatural aid he receives, we must first appreciate the character of John the Baptist. It is difficult to overestimate John's importance in Luke's narrative. As we discussed in chapter 2, it is not only Jesus who has a miraculous birth, foretold by angels, but John as well. John's remarkable birth is only the beginning of the long-term role he will have in Luke's two-volume narrative.

At the beginning of chapter 3, we meet John as an adult. Once again, Luke is interested in placing his tale in the context of political and world history.

> In the fifteenth year of the reign of Tiberius Caesar—when Pontius Pilate was governor of Judea, Herod tetrarch of Galilee, his brother Philip tetrarch of Iturea and Traconitis, and Lysanias tetrarch of Abilene—during the high-priesthood of Annas and Caiaphas, the word of God came to John son of Zechariah in the wilderness. (Luke 3:1-2)

We learned previously (1:80) that John lived in the wilderness; now "the word of God" comes to John in said wilderness, similar to Elijah (1 Kgs 19).[3] All four Gospels understand John's ministry in light of Isa 40. Luke includes the following:

---

2. Some later versions of the Hero's Journey talk about this phase as the meeting of the mentor instead of supernatural aid, the former being a more general category of aid given to the hero. See Vogler, *Writer's Journey*.

3. While Matthew and Mark both specifically describe John's clothing (Matt 3:4, Mark 1:6), which is a clear homage to Elijah (2 Kgs 1:1-8), Luke omits this. Luke will also distance Jesus's ministry from that of Elijah (Luke 9:52-26). Nolland holds that both contemporary and traditional Jewish understanding envision eschatological renewal beginning in the wilderness (*Luke 1:1—9:20*, 145).

Part 1: Departure

> A voice of one calling in the wilderness,
> "Prepare the way for the Lord,
>   make straight paths for him.
> Every valley shall be filled in,
>   every mountain and hill made low.
> The crooked roads shall become straight,
>   the rough ways smooth.
> And all people will see God's salvation."
> (Luke 3:4b–6, quoting Isa 40:3–5)

This passage is significant. Not only does it speak of preparing the way of the Lord, a role the angel told Zechariah John would have (1:17), and end with a distinctly Lukan theme—"all people will see God's salvation"—but this is a significant reference in the book of Isaiah. Isaiah 40 starts the second part of Isaiah (40–66)—often referred to by scholars as Second Isaiah—where the story shifts to focusing more directly on a vision of restoration and salvation.[4] The first words of Isa 40 are "Comfort, comfort my people." Likewise, Jesus's first declarations about himself will be from Second Isaiah (Isa 61).[5]

In addition, John has a prophetic teaching ministry of his own. While Luke will be concerned with presenting Jesus as the primary prophetic figure in Luke, John is a worthy forerunner.[6] John's language and imagery can be confusing, but the central component of his charge to the crowds seems to be "Produce fruit in keeping with repentance" (Luke 3:8) or, in other words, *prove that you are changing by how you live*. This is followed by a string of practical advice John gives to certain groups who ask how they should respond.

---

4. By contrast, the enduring image of Isa 1–9 is that of trees being cut down, leaving only stumps. See Isa 6:13.

5. While it goes beyond the scope of this work, there is an important scholarly discussion regarding Luke's use of Isaiah, namely, the new exodus. For more on this study, see Fox, *Hermeneutics of Social Identity*, 89–93; Beers, *Followers of Jesus*; Pao, *Isaianic New Exodus*.

6. That word "prophetic" can be misunderstood, as for some it has become synonymous with "predict the future." While certain prophecies can and do have a futuristic element (i.e., foretelling)—indeed, the messianic prophesies about the future, the angelic predictions about John and Jesus, etc. are some of the most famous—by far the most common usage of that word in the Scripture and in scholarship refers to speaking God's word in the present (i.e., forthtelling). See Fee and Stuart, *How to Read Bible*, 188. For a definition of "the prophetic" in Luke-Acts, based on previous textual evidence, see Johnson, *Gospel of Luke*, 17–19.

John's impact on the crowds is significant enough that they wonder if he could be the messiah (3:15), a claim he quickly and readily denies in deference to Jesus (3:15–17), who has yet to come on the scene. By the end of chapter 3, we learn that John challenges Herod for his evil deeds and gets sent to prison. Luke does not narrate his execution, but lest one think that putting John in prison will mitigate his influence, Luke shows us the character's continued impact in his story—perhaps like Ben Kenobi. John continues to be a regular point of comparison throughout the story. Jesus is questioned about fasting, and the Pharisees compare him and his disciples to John and John's disciples (5:33). Then we have a key scene in chapter 7 where John, from prison, sends his disciples to ask Jesus if he is the one who is to come or if should they wait for another. This is a heightened scene of irony that we often overlook or miss: the prophetic figure who comes to prepare the way for Jesus is now uncertain if Jesus is the one.

Commentaries discuss the options in play here. Jesus's ministry in chapter 7 is a ministry of healing and resurrection (7:1–17), not the fiery figure bringing judgment with the axe at the root of the tree John envisioned. Jesus is not a new Elijah; rather than simply replicating the ministry of Elijah, Jesus surpasses him (7:11–17). Instead, Jesus is a Messiah in the spirit of Isaiah's vision. Jesus's response shows how his ministry is defined: "The blind receive sight, the lame walk, those who have leprosy are cleansed, the deaf hear, the dead are raised, and the good news is proclaimed to the poor. Blessed is anyone who does not stumble on account of me" (7:22–23).

Jesus continues to discuss his significant role after John's disciples leave. According to Jesus, John is "more than a prophet" and "among those born of women no one is greater than John" (7:28). The people, having been baptized by John, agree, but the Pharisees "rejected God's purposes for themselves, because they had not been baptized by John" (7:30). John's baptism becomes something of a litmus test for recognition of and participation in the new move of God that is happening in the coming of Jesus. This call back to the ministry of John will continue for the remainder of Luke and even into Acts.[7] John's baptism is considered "the beginning" (Acts 1:22), it is referenced at Cornelius' house (Acts 10:37), and even as late as Acts 18–19, Apollos, along with some others in Ephesus, does not know of the Holy Spirit but only of the baptism of John. To consider that Apollos, a Jew from Alexandria, who is in Ephesus, along with others, knows of the baptism of John decades later and over a thousand miles away testifies to

---

7. Luke 9:7, 19; 11:1; 16:16; 20:4.

PART 1: DEPARTURE

John's formidable impact. On the story level we are meant to remember John as the significant figure with whom the new move of God started.

John Truby, in his seminal book on storytelling, suggests that the key to presenting great characters in literature and film is their interrelatedness to each other.[8] The best characters are created by connecting and comparing them to others. We understand the hero through his or her connection to other characters. John and Jesus work well as an example of this in Luke. John has a significant ministry of his own: he draws crowds, he has a prophetic teaching ministry, he proclaims the good news to them. Despite all this, when the people ask if he is the messiah, he readily defers to the one coming after him, Jesus. Through this comparison we are able to fully appreciate the ministry of Jesus.

Since John's ministry of baptism and Jesus's temptation—both in view in the current chapter—occur in a wilderness setting, a deeper look at the role of wilderness is needed.

What Is the Role of the Wilderness in Luke-Acts?

The wilderness, the desert, has an interesting role in both human history and the history of storytelling. First, it is a dry and desolate place, filled with danger and scarcity. Without the ability to grow crops and have access to water, survival in the wilderness is tumultuous. For this reason, the Old Testament at times talks about the wilderness as "vast and dreadful," a "thirsty and waterless land, filled with snakes and scorpions" (Deut 8:15). It is a dangerous liminal space that people travel through out of necessity but not normally as their first choice. It is even at times associated with evil and the demonic, where the scapegoat carrying the sins of the people is sent and where nefarious people dwell (Lev 16). Similarly, Campbell notices the trend in numerous stories around the world, saying that they "populate with deceitful and dangerous presences every desert place outside the normal traffic of the village."[9]

However, we cannot forget that perhaps the key event in the formation of Israel as a people was the exodus from Egyptian slavery and the subsequent wondering in the wilderness. This becomes a dominant metaphor in the biblical witness that looms large over so many references. Thus, the wilderness is not only a dangerous place, it is ironically also a place of

---

8. Truby, *Anatomy of Story*, 56–57.
9. Campbell, *Hero with a Thousand Faces*, 78.

refuge. It is a place to which those who are in peril in the city flee for safety (1 Sam 23:14; 1 Kgs 19:4).

Luke does not correct the image of the wilderness being wild and untamed. A boy possessed by demons is driven from the tombs into the wilderness (Luke 8:26–29). Jesus's disciples become aware of their scarcity of food in the wilderness, leading to the miraculous feeding of five thousand people (9:12). In Jesus's parable of the lost sheep, the sheep will become lost in the wilderness (15:4). But despite these references to danger and evil, the wilderness in Luke-Acts is also a place of spiritual renewal, where the moving of God starts. We see the ironic juxtaposition of danger, scarcity, and evil up against profound prophetic activity from a character said to live in the wilderness. John's quote from Isa 40 uses wilderness imagery, which Luke extends the passage to include:

> Every valley shall be filled in,
>   every mountain and hill made low.
> The crooked roads shall become straight,
>   the rough ways smooth. (Luke 3:5–6)

This fits with Luke's emphasis on God's justice we see expounded on in other places, such as the song of Mary and John the Baptist's instructions to those being baptized. Indeed, John the Baptist is a figure specifically connected with the wilderness. But John is not alone. Jesus, too, will venture into the wilderness, specifically for his showdown with the devil. But he will also withdraw to the wilderness to pray (4:42; 5:16).

JESUS'S BAPTISM

As others are being baptized, Jesus is baptized too. Luke's description of what happens at Jesus's baptism is fairly short. Nonetheless, it is where we see the significant supernatural aid bestowed on Jesus:

> When all the people were being baptized, Jesus was baptized too. And as he was praying, heaven was opened and the Holy Spirit descended on him in bodily form like a dove. And a voice came from heaven: "You are my Son, whom I love; with you I am well pleased." (3:21–22)

This scene introduces two key elements of supernatural aid our hero possesses throughout the rest of the story. The first is a special relationship with the Father. We saw this already when the angel announced the birth of Jesus, saying he will be "called the Son of God" (1:35), and when the boy Jesus was found in the temple, his "Father's house" (2:49). He will prioritize times of prayer (Luke 4:42; 5:16), refer to coming in the glory of his Father (9:26), and state that his Father has committed all things to him (10:22) and conferred to him a kingdom (22:29). This special relationship between the Father and Jesus is an essential part of what makes Jesus heroic and special in Luke.

But it is not the only thing, nor is it the most prominent. For Luke, the Holy Spirit is a more ubiquitous force. We must be careful not to project back into these early Gospel texts the later theological category of the Trinity. While I affirm the truth and importance of the Trinitarian nature of God in three persons, Father, Son, and Holy Spirit, as rightly affirmed from Scripture at the Council of Nicaea, the original readers were not thinking in those neatly defined theological terms.

I see this in my students sometimes, where they allow later theological categories to undercut the story. For example, in John when Jesus raises Lazarus from the dead, students will sometimes react, saying, "Well yeah, Jesus is God, so of course he can raise someone from the dead." Okay, but to take that approach is to miss the marvelous wonder that is Lazarus having been dead for four days and then walking out of the grave in his graveclothes! Don't let anything ruin the story. Stay in the story, with the author and on the author's terms. That is key here as well.

The Holy Spirit is not a new character on the scene at Jesus's baptism. The Holy Spirit was said to fill John before he was born (1:15), to come upon Mary for the conception of Jesus (1:35), to fill Elizabeth when she hears Mary's voice, to fill Zechariah as he sings his song (1:67), and to prompt Simeon that he would see the Messiah (2:26). The Holy Spirit is a significant part of the coming of Jesus and starting of his ministry. A few references will continue in the rest of Luke, but Acts will be the ultimate culmination of the continued presence of Jesus in the form of the Holy Spirit. In Luke-Acts the Holy Spirit is not limited to Jesus but, rather, is promised and available to all believers. While Jesus's special relationship with the Father is unique to him, the Holy Spirit is available to all.

It is in the power of the Holy Spirit that Jesus ventures into the wilderness to be tempted by Satan.

Supernatural Aid

TEMPTATION IN THE WILDERNESS

Some of the early phases of the Hero's Journey—the call to adventure, supernatural aid, crossing the threshold—blend together in Luke's Gospel. Jesus's baptism might be thought of as his call to adventure, his venture into the wilderness to be tempted by Satan may well fit as the crossing-the-threshold phase. I am including the temptation here, in the discussion of supernatural aid, as we see him immediately put that aid to the test. Further, I think it best to see his sermon in Nazareth as crossing the threshold, which we will talk about next chapter.

At Jesus's baptism, the voice from heaven declares to Jesus, "You are my beloved Son, whom I love" (paraphrased from Luke 3:22). Luke then recounts Jesus's genealogy, which connects him to key characters such as David and Abraham but most importantly Adam, ending the section stating that Adam was the son of God, reinforcing that Jesus is the Son of God. Luke then tells us, "Jesus, full of the Holy Spirit, left the Jordan and was led by the Holy Spirit into the wilderness where for forty days he was tempted by the Devil" (Luke 4:1–2a). The temptations will seek to challenge the identity just established that Jesus is the Son of God.[10]

Campbell was heavily influenced by the work of psychologist Carl Jung, who understood human behavior, including the stories we tell, through a number of certain archetypes. He imagined these archetypes as part of a larger web of knowledge and imagery shared by all people that he called "the collective unconscious."[11] These archetypes show up in the Hero's Journey and in stories around the world. There is an obvious connection with one of Jung's archetypes here, as we can understand the devil in the wilderness as a form of Jung's trickster figure.[12] This trickster figure is often known for "his fondness for sly jokes and malicious pranks," as well as "his approximation to the figure of a savior."[13]

We have such a scene here in the wilderness. The trickster, the devil, comes to Jesus when he is weak and tries to trick him. This scene and this foe stand at the threshold of Jesus's public ministry,[14] and the Synoptic Gospels all see this as a crucial confrontation that needs to take place before

---

10. Parsons, *Luke*, 70.
11. Jung, *Archetypes of Collective Unconscious*, 3–4.
12. Jung, *Archetypes of Collective Unconscious*, 255–74.
13. Jung, *Archetypes of Collective Unconscious*, 255.
14. Parsons, *Luke*, 70.

Part 1: Departure

Jesus's public ministry can start. Indeed, it is the Spirit who leads Jesus into the wilderness for this encounter (4:1).

The temptations of Jesus in Luke move from the desert floor, to a high place, to the pinnacle of the temple, that is, a movement "up to Jerusalem" that will be mirrored by Jesus in the last two-thirds of the Gospel. That movement—a key structural feature for Luke-Acts as a whole—is prefigured here.[15]

Each of the temptations serves to question Jesus's identity, the first and third specifically starting with the phrase "If you are the Son of God." Jesus, in the wilderness forty days, experiences the same tests as Israel, in the wilderness forty years: hunger (Exod 16), idolatry (Exod 32), and doubting God's faithfulness (Exod 17).[16] Where Israel failed, Jesus succeeds. The supernatural aid he received at his baptism, specifically his confirmed identity as the Son of God and the presence of the Holy Spirit, help him to overcome the temptations. In addition, though, we see Jesus quote Scripture in response to each of these temptations. Scripture works as a type of "utility belt" for Jesus to use in this scenario, even when the devil uses Scripture to try to trip him up. The Matthew scene ends with Jesus commanding the devil to leave; by contrast, Luke shows the devil leaving him "for an opportune time" (Luke 4:13). At least for the moment, the threshold guardian, the trickster figure, has been bested.

Having received supernatural aid from his Father and the Holy Spirit, and having bested the threshold guardian, Jesus is now ready to cross the threshold into his public ministry. But that is never pleasant. Transitioning from one world to the next is challenging and uncomfortable. It is with this in mind that we look at Jesus first public teaching in Luke—the Nazareth sermon.

---

15. This material comes from the Q source; while Mark has a temptation scene, he does not describe the specific temptations. Matthew and Luke have the same temptations but in a different order. Scholarly consensus holds Matthew's order as original (Parsons, *Luke*, 72), which leads us to ask why Luke changes the order. I hold that this movement—desert floor, high place, pinnacle of the temple—better fits with Luke's larger theme of geographical progression in Luke-Acts.

16. Parsons, *Luke*, 71. Israel is also called God's son in Exod 4:22, an image that continues throughout the Old Testament (Hos 11:1; Mic 5:1–3; etc.).

Supernatural Aid

DISCUSSION QUESTIONS

1. Do you feel that John the Baptist and the significance of his ministry get overlooked? If so, why?
2. Which scenes from books or movies can you think of that occur in the desert/wilderness? What is the significance of that setting in those scenes?
3. Why do you think the Gospels all see Jesus's temptation by Satan as so significant?

4

Crossing the Threshold

The crossing of the threshold is the first step into the sacred zone of the universal source.
—Joseph Campbell, *The Hero with a Thousand Faces*, 81

[Jesus] came to Nazareth where he had been raised. As he always did on the Sabbath, he went to the meeting place.
—Luke 4:16 MSG

THE JOURNEY OF EVERY hero involves a quest, a departure from the mundane world they know in search of something more. This can look many different ways, such as Aladdin seeking the lamp, or humans stealing fire from Prometheus, or the specific character MacGuffins from *The Wizard of Oz*. This quest involves a departure, an embarkation, a crossing of the threshold into the journey of the hero.

Jesus crosses a threshold as well. Before he crosses this threshold, Jesus appears to be simply a local Galilean Jew, private, pedestrian, and in solidarity with the people going out to John for baptism. After his threshold-crossing experience, Jesus becomes a public figure and a prophet. This threshold is not in a faraway land or the murky edge of a dark and dangerous forest but, ironically, in his hometown, with his own people. It is there that Jesus begins to take on his prophetic role and challenge the bounds of the status quo. Campbell says:

> One had better not challenge the watcher of the established bounds. And yet—it is only by advancing beyond those bounds, provoking the destructive other aspect of the same power, that the individual passes, either alive or in death, into a new zone of experience. . . . The adventure is always and everywhere a passage beyond the veil of the known into the unknown; the powers that watch at the boundary are dangerous; to deal with them is risky; yet for anyone with competence and courage the danger fades.[1]

Jesus goes to his home synagogue, ready to challenge the established bounds. Luke is careful to tell us at the beginning of the scene that he is "in the power of the Spirit" and that "everyone praised him" (4:15-16). He is handed the scroll to read; we are again in the redemptive world envisioned by the prophet Isaiah. Luke gives this story a flair of dramatic detail, which slows down the pace of the scene. He reports that Jesus stood to read; we can visualize the scroll being handed to him, then Jesus finding his place and reading:

> The Spirit of the Lord is on me,
>   because he has anointed me
> to proclaim good news to the poor.
> He has sent me to proclaim freedom for the prisoners
>   and recovery of sight for the blind,
> to set the oppressed free,
> to proclaim the year of the Lord's favor.
> (4:18-19, quoting Isa 61:1-2, with a phrase borrowed from Isa 58:6)

Likewise after the reading, Luke continues with the dramatic flair, noting that Jesus hands back the scroll to the attendant and sits down, and all the eyes are on him. "Today this scripture is fulfilled in your hearing" (Luke 4:21). The initial reaction of the synagogue attendees is positive; they "were amazed" at his gracious words. "Isn't this Joseph's son?" they ask, a positive statement of pride that one of their own is pronouncing God's favor on the people (4:22). We see the specific emphasis here of Jesus's ministry focus to the poor, blind, and enslaved, in Jubilee terms.[2] The people

---

1. Campbell, *Hero with a Thousand Faces*, 82.
2. I contend that Jesus is intentionally using Jubilee language here, which will unfold

at the synagogue must have assumed they would have a privileged place in this outpouring of God's favor.[3] But like John before him, Jesus is a prophet, and he comes with a challenging prophetic message. This hero is here to challenge what it means to be in God's family.

JESUS'S ROLE AS PROPHET

Key to appreciating the heroic quest of Jesus in Luke is understanding Jesus's role as a prophet. Some have a mistaken understanding of the word "prophet" as one who predicts the future. This is a pervasive use of the word in modern parlance, but the biblical idea of prophecy, as well as the biblical role of a prophet, is much more robust and nuanced. While there are certain prophecies that have a futuristic element, predicting the future is an extremely small part of what the prophet does.[4] By far the most common usage of that word in Scripture involves embodying a specific role among the Israelites. This role of prophet involved three primary parts, with a fourth coming from the response of others. Luke clearly and intentionally presents Jesus this way in Luke-Acts. These elements are primarily patterned after the first and greatest prophet in Hebrew tradition, Moses.[5] Indeed, the Hebrew people looked forward to a day that God would raise up a prophet like Moses (Deut 18:15), a verse specifically referenced in Acts 7:37. Moses is described as one who "the Lord knew face to face . . . who did all those signs and wonders" among the people (Deut 34:10–12).[6] Let's examine the elements of a prophet as Luke presents them.

---

over the course of his ministry and be fulfilled in the community in Acts, specifically in texts such as Acts 2:42–47; 4:32–35. I am currently editing an article called "Jubilee in Luke-Acts" for future publication that will address this more fully.

3. Parsons, *Luke*, 81–83.

4. That the most famous prophecies in Scripture, such as the messianic prophesies, the angelic predictions about John, Jesus, etc. are futuristic reinforces this false notion. Fee and Stuart estimate that only 5 percent of prophecy in the Old Testament has this future orientation into the new covenant age (*How to Read Bible*, 188). As Heschel eloquently puts it, "While it is true that foretelling is an important ingredient and may serve as a sign of the prophet's authority (Deut 18:22; Isa 41:22; 43:9), his essential task is to declare the word of God to the here and now" (*Prophets*, 14–15). For a definition of "the prophetic" in Luke-Acts, based on previous textual evidence, see Johnson, *Gospel of Luke*, 17–19.

5. Johnson, *Gospel of Luke*, 18. Johnson cites Ps 78:11–12, 32, 43.

6. Per Johnson, these expectations remained alive in first-century Judaism (*Gospel of Luke*, 18). See 4Q175 1–5 and John 1:21; 4:19; 6:14.

1. The Prophet Is Filled with the Holy Spirit

Moses had a special relationship with God. The Torah describes Moses as speaking face to face with God numerous times, denoting a special relationship between the two.[7] Moses is also regularly connected with the Holy Spirit in his leadership and prophetic role.[8] In Num 11, for example, Moses is part of dispensing the Spirit that is on him to others who might help bear the burden of leadership. Likewise, Luke is clear to establish both of these qualities in the life of Jesus. Jesus's birth is a clear indication of his special relationship with the Father, as he is said to be "great and will be called the Son of the Most High. The Lord will give him the throne of his father David and he will reign over Jacob's descendants forever; his kingdom will never end" (Luke 1:33). Jesus also refers to God as his Father (2:49). These indications demonstrate Jesus's messianic role as a prophet like Moses. Jesus is also said to be filled with the Holy Spirit. The association with the Holy Spirit becomes Luke's most common way of describing this prophetic connection. As stated previously, while only Jesus has the special connection to the Father reserved for the Messiah, many characters are said to have the Holy Spirit.[9] The Spirit descends on Jesus as a dove (3:22), he goes into the wilderness full of the Holy Spirit (4:1), and he enters Nazareth in the power of the Spirit (4:14). The key characters in Acts continue this prophetic pattern. Johnson says, "The characters in Acts who fundamentally advance the plot . . . are not *called* prophets . . . instead, Luke describes his main characters in stereotypical language which clearly demarcates them as prophets."[10] Nonetheless, this prophetic role is most prominent and most clearly seen in Jesus.

2. The Prophet Proclaims the Message of God

A second element of the role of the prophet for Jesus is proclaiming the message or word of God, specifically in his time, the good news, or gospel. Being a spokesperson for God is an important role for the prophet. Modern Jewish scholarship helpfully describes the teaching ministry of the

---

7. Exod 33:11; Num 12:7–8; Deut 5:4; 34:10.
8. Num 11:17–29; Ps 106:33; Neh 9:10.
9. Luke 1:15, 35, 67; 2:25–26; Acts 4:8; 5:32; 6:3; 7:55; 11:24; 13:9.
10. Johnson, *Gospel of Luke*, 17; emphasis in original. They are said to be filled with the Holy Spirit in Acts 4:8; 5:32; 6:3; 7:55; 11:24; 13:9.

prophets as the "exegesis of existence from a divine perspective."[11] Indeed, Moses was the spokesperson for God to the wilderness community, having been given the holy words of God.[12] Likewise, regarding the prophet like Moses in Deut 18:18, God says, "I will put my words in his mouth." Spirit-inspired speech was a key element of the concept of the prophet in the Hebrew Scriptures.[13] The "word of God" and "preaching the good news" are both essential elements of Jesus's ministry introduced early and reinforced throughout.[14] Jesus is said to teach with authority (Luke 4:32) and to be mighty in word and deed (24:19). More than simply being described in this way, Jesus clearly demonstrates each of these in his ministry. This teaching and proclaiming element of the prophet role will continue throughout Acts, with an emphasis on boldness.[15] The teaching of Jesus will go beyond simply the proclaiming of a simple message but instead will cover many different areas of life viewed through the perspective of God's kingdom.

3. The Prophet Works Signs and Wonders Among the People

The third element is the working of signs and wonders, something that Moses is specifically said to have done in Deut 34:12. Likewise, one of the most recognizable features of Jesus's ministry will be this working of signs and wonders; it will cause amazement in the people and will draw large crowds. This will primarily begin to happen with specific emphasis in his Galilean ministry but will continue throughout his public ministry and up to his final week. The working of miracles will continue with the apostles in Acts as well.[16]

In these three ways, Jesus enacts the role of the prophet like Moses and sets forth his heroic path and his role as the redeemer. The apostles in Acts will play similar roles following in Jesus's footsteps, continuing the ministry of Jesus in each of these three ways as enabled by his enduring presence. However, there is one more element of this prophetic task that needs exploration. It is not something that Jesus says or does but, rather, the way others respond to him, as they did to the prophets before him.

11. Heschel, *Prophets*, xxvii.
12. Acts 7:38; Exod 4.
13. Deut 34:9; Isa 42:1; 43:3; 48:16; 59:21; 61:1–4.
14. Luke 4:18, 43; 5:1; 7:22; 8:1, 11; 9:6; 11:28; 16:16; 20:1.
15. Acts 4:13, 29; 5:42; 8:4, 12, 14, 25, 40; 11:20; 13:5, 32, 46; 14:7; 15:35; 28:31.
16. Acts 4:30; 6:8; 8:6; 14:3; 15:12.

4. The Prophet Is Rejected

A common element of the prophetic task is that prophets and their message are rejected by the people. The people rejected Moses, crafting other gods and desiring to return to Egypt.[17] Elijah is rejected and on the run, and other prophets are regularly persecuted, all because of the prophetic message they bring.[18] For Luke, this is a key feature of recognizing Jesus in his prophetic role. Jesus is rejected by specific groups of people and will make specific mention of this several times in his ministry.[19] It is important to note that not all of the people reject Jesus. Jesus regularly teaches and ministers to vast crowds of people who hang on Jesus's every word up until the last week of his life (Luke 19:48). This crowd makes it difficult for the ones who do reject him, "the chief priests, the teachers of the law, and the leaders," to arrest him and kill him (19:47).[20] But the ultimate rejection of Jesus is his arrest and crucifixion. Although he is rejected by people, he is vindicated by God, a pattern of proclamation we see numerous times in Acts.[21]

There is a literary, perhaps rhetorical, function in Luke with regard to how people respond to Jesus. In essentially every subgroup of people we encounter in Luke, some receive him and some reject him. Whether it is disciples, rich people, Roman soldiers, thieves on the cross, or members of the Sanhedrin, Luke portrays some as receptive to Jesus's message and others as unreceptive.[22] No matter the subgroup a person is in, this prophet demands a decision. We recognize Luke's rhetorical challenge to the reader: no matter who you are, you must make a decision about Jesus and his prophetic message.

---

17. Exod 32:1–6, 23; Num 14:3–4; 16:13; Acts 7:35–42.

18. 1 Kgs 19; Jer 1; Acts 7:35, 39; Heb 11:32–38.

19. Luke 4:24; 6:23; 9:22; 11:47–50; 13:33–34; 17:25; 18:31–33; 20:17; Acts 4:11; 7:35, 39.

20. The people generally love and welcome Jesus and his prophetic ministry. The exceptions fall into three groups, that is, the extremely religious, the powerful, and the rich. These three groups regularly clash with Jesus because he brings a challenging and iconoclastic message about the things those groups hold dear.

21. Luke 2:23, 36; 3:13–18; 10:39.

22. Luke 7:1–10; 22:1–6; 18:18–30; 19:1–10; 23:36, 39–43, 50–56.

Part 1: Departure

RESPONSE AT NAZARETH

Jesus reads Isa 61 and declares that the Scripture is fulfilled; an apt crossing-the-threshold moment, leaving the mundane world of an inconspicuous figure for the public life of an itinerant prophet. Indeed, each of the elements of his prophetic role—Spirit of the Lord upon him, proclaiming good news, and reference to signs and wonders (i.e., proclaim release, sight for blind, etc.)—is represented in the passage. The fourth element will come in the people's response to him.

After the people marvel at Jesus's gracious words, Jesus references two stories from the Hebrew Scriptures. In the first, during a time of drought, Elijah the prophet was sent to the widow of Zarephath, not to Israelites (1 Kgs 17:7–24). In the second story, Elisha the prophet was sent to a leper, once again, not to any of the lepers in Israel but rather to Naaman the Syrian (2 Kgs 5:1–19a). Like these Old Testament prophets, Jesus's ministry will be for all people, not exclusively Israel and not delimited to his hometown. Rather, because of Jesus's ministry "all people will see God's salvation" (Luke 3:6). This inclusive message "wins him no friends among his own people."[23] Luke tells us that the people were furious. The crowd that was so recently marveling at his words now drag him to a cliff, intending to kill him (4:29).

Again we see that the Holy Spirit has led Jesus into the realm of conflict and danger, as previously with the showdown with the devil in the wilderness. Lest we think the Holy Spirit's primary emphasis is safety and comfort, that notion is dispelled quickly and thoroughly. This truth will be on display in the rest of Luke's Gospel and continue to be emphasized in Acts, where virtually every prominent Christian leader will be arrested, beaten, and/or killed for their participation in Jesus's movement.[24] The Hero's Journey is fraught with danger. Indeed, persecution is the norm in Luke-Acts for the follower of Jesus.

That brings us to another significant phase of the Hero's Journey: the road of trials. Having crossed the threshold from inconspicuous citizen to public prophet in Nazareth, Jesus's ministry, his quest, is under way. The road of trials begins in the form of the Galilean ministry. To those encounters we now turn.

---

23. Parsons, *Luke*, 83.

24. Stephen (Acts 6:1—8:1), Peter (3–5; 12:3–19), James (12:1–3), Paul (9:29–30; 14:19–20; 16:16–40; 19:20–34; 21:27–36).

Crossing the Threshold

DISCUSSION QUESTIONS

1. What other scenes from books and movies can you think of that feature a dramatic crossing-the-threshold experience for the character?
2. Why do you think the people in Nazareth rejected Jesus so profoundly?
3. What experiences in your own life could you consider a crossing of a threshold into a new phase or journey?

PART 2

Initiation

Once having traversed the threshold, the hero moves in a dream landscape of curiously fluid, ambiguous forms, where he must survive a succession of trials. This is a favorite phase of the myth adventure.
—Joseph Campbell, *The Hero with a Thousand Faces*, 97

5

The Hero's Companions

Another function of this stage is the making of Allies and Enemies. It is natural for heroes just arriving in the Special World to spend some time figuring out who can be trusted and relied upon for special services, and who is not to be trusted.
—Christopher Vogler, *The Writer's Journey*, 161

At about that same time he climbed a mountain to pray. He was there all night in prayer before God. The next day he summoned his disciples; from them he selected twelve he designated as apostles.
—Luke 6:12-13 MSG

ONE OF THE MOST distinctive marks of the Hero's Journey is the inclusion of companions on the journey. Luke Skywalker is joined by Han Solo, Chewbacca, Princess Leia, and occasionally others. Frodo has his faithful friend Sam Gamgee, as well as the other members of the fellowship. Don Quixote has the comically witty Sancho Panza at his side. Companions are an important part of the journey who can help tell the story more fully. Similarly, heroes also have enemies, those who arise in the story to try to thwart the character's goals.

Part 2: Initiation

Jesus also had both allies and enemies on his journey, and they make for a critically important element of this hero's story. Jesus interacts with the Twelve, who follow him as his itinerant disciples. While Peter and sometimes John play more prominent roles in the group, Judas has a crucial role as the betrayer. But there are other key companions as well, including John the Baptist, the women disciples who follow Jesus and play crucial roles in the narrative, the larger group of disciples who follow Jesus, and the crowds.

A FIRST LOOK AT COMPANIONS

In the last chapter we talked about John the Baptist and his importance in Luke's narrative. To say here only briefly, John is a critically important character in the narrative, preparing the way for Jesus and setting the stage narratively for the coming of Jesus. He is a companion of Jesus in that he baptizes Jesus and affirms him as the Son of God. However, since by the end of chapter 3 John is imprisoned by Herod, he does not function as a companion of Jesus for most of the narrative.

Christopher Booker, in his book *The Seven Basic Plots*, talks about the different roles companions can play in hero stories. First, companions can be "undifferentiated appendages," where the companions may be a group whose names we may not even know. Second, a companion might be a faithful alter ego. Third, a companion could play the role of an alter ego who works as a foil, contrasting to and counteracting the hero. Fourth, companions can work as a group where the members each have distinct characteristics adding up to a whole.[1] In Luke, the primary companions of Jesus include the twelve disciples, with Peter and Judas as notable standouts, as well as the women—a too often overlooked group who play an essential role in the story—and the larger group of disciples beyond the Twelve. We will look at each of these in turn.

THE TWELVE

The disciples are the most well-known companions of Jesus in Luke. Luke narrates the calling of Simon Peter (Luke 5:1–11), along with the sons of Zebedee, who are relegated to one verse at the end of the calling of Peter

---

1. Booker, *Seven Basic Plots*, 72.

The Hero's Companions

(5:10),[2] as well as the calling of Levi (5:27–32). Levi's story is not developed more fully, but his calling and the party he has with his tax collector friends for Jesus allow an opportunity for Jesus to clarify his mission. The full list of Twelve is given in Luke 6:13–16:[3]

> When morning came, he called his disciples to him and chose twelve of them, whom he also designated apostles: Simon (whom he named Peter), his brother Andrew, James, John, Philip, Bartholomew, Matthew, Thomas, James son of Alphaeus, Simon who was called the Zealot, Judas son of James, and Judas Iscariot, who became a traitor.

Peter plays the role of the most prominent of and spokesperson for the disciples in Luke (and all of the canonical Gospels).

Booker's categories above are helpful for us to understand the roles of the Twelve. For the most part, they are a group of undifferentiated appendages; without the list of their names in 6:13–16, we would not know most of their names. Two disciples stand out from the group, however. Simon Peter might be seen as a combination of Booker's categories 2 and 3. First, he is sometimes a faithful alter ego who is primarily noted for his fidelity. He will serve as a spokesperson and leader for the Twelve, doing tasks such as preparing the Last Supper at Jesus's command (19:28–33), and will also have the opportunity to confess Jesus as the Messiah before the journey to Jerusalem (9:18–20). However, more often, Peter serves as a foil for Jesus. He is not evil or an enemy of the Lord, but he does regularly represent a viewpoint contrary to Jesus. He points out oddities and allows Jesus to clarify. For example, in Luke 8, Jesus is surrounded by a great crowd, and the woman with the issue of blood touches the hem of his garment and Jesus feels the power flow out of him (8:40–48). Peter says, "Master, the people are crowding and pressing against you." Peter points out the strangeness of what Jesus says; with such a great crowd, how can he be particular about being touched by someone? And yet, it is this pushback that gives Jesus the opportunity in the narrative to identify the woman and commend her faith. Similarly, in chapter 18, after the encounter with the rich man, Peter is the one who points out, "We have left all we had to follow you!"

---

2. Matthew and Mark give slightly longer narrations of the calling of James and John. Luke likely focuses on Peter because of the role Peter will play in Acts.

3. Luke offers no statement of purpose like we see in Mark 3:14, which says, "He appointed them that they might be with him and that he might send them out to preach."

(18:28). Again, Jesus is able to clarify the kingdom rewards for those who leave earthly pleasures to follow him.[4]

Despite playing this sort of a foil character for Jesus in Luke, Peter has a noteworthy character arc in Luke-Acts. It also introduces the reader to his twofold role of the alter ego, both faithful and foil. The first time we meet Peter he is fishing, and after a full night, he (along with his unnamed companions) allows Jesus to use his boat to teach the crowd. After this, Jesus tells Simon to go into deep water and cast the nets. Peter replies, "Master, we've worked hard all night and haven't caught anything. But because you say so, I will let down the nets" (Luke 5:5). Here we see both his pushback, stating the uncommon nature of Jesus's request but also his faithfulness. The result—such a large catch that the nets begin to break and partners have to bring the other boat to help—causes Peter to fall at Jesus's feet, saying, "Go away from me, Lord; I am a sinful man!" (5:8). With ups and downs throughout the Gospel, including famously denying Jesus three times (22:58–61) despite his insistence that he will remain faithful (22:33), Peter is truly a picture of the transforming nature of Jesus. He will become the spokesperson for the early group of disciples in Acts, preaching at Pentecost (Acts 2), displaying great boldness before the Sanhedrin (Acts 3–5), and helping facilitate the inclusion of gentiles into the move of God (Acts 10–11).[5]

The other famous—or infamous—member of the Twelve is Judas, who will ultimately betray Jesus. We may see Judas in something of a foil role to Jesus as well, but it is much different than the presentation of Peter. The reader knows from chapter 6 that Judas will be the one to betray Jesus, as upon introduction, the narrator introduces him as "Judas Iscariot, who became a traitor" (Luke 6:16). He is not mentioned again until 22:3 when Luke tells the reader that Satan entered Judas. Unlike the other Gospels,

---

4. Another similar scene where Peter plays this sort of role is at the transfiguration in 9:32–33.

5. Peter is undoubtedly a prominent figure in the first part of Acts, and some even argue that there is reason to believe that Acts is comparing him and his role to Jesus in various ways, primarily as a miracle worker, leader of the community, and interpreter of Scripture and events (not as a new Messiah figure). Both his successes and failures in Luke prepare Peter to carry on the mission after Jesus. It is worth noting that three famous scenes from other canonical Gospels involving Peter are absent from Luke: Peter walking on water, cutting the ear off of the servant at Jesus's arrest—the Synoptics all mention this scene, but none of them identifies this disciple as Peter, as John will—and Peter rebuking Jesus for saying he will die in Jerusalem and Jesus responding with "Get behind me, Satan."

Judas has no role in Luke other than the betrayal. He works as a foil for Jesus only in the sense that he turns an innocent Jesus over to those who seek to kill him. For that reason, he is important in the narrative as he helps with the dramatic unfolding of the final week.[6] He has no speaking lines in the narrative, and Luke does not even include his death in the Gospel; he instead saves that for the beginning of Acts, when they are choosing a replacement, so he can further elaborate on Judas' demise.[7]

THE WOMEN

Luke is careful to intentionally include women in his narrative. One way this happens is by pairing male and female characters, such as with the songs of Mary and Zechariah, Simeon and Anna, and healing stories (i.e., a demon-possessed man in 4:31–37 and Peter's mother-in-law in 4:38–39).[8] It also happens by making a specific group of female disciples crucially important to the story.

We learn in 8:1–3:

> After this, Jesus traveled about from one town and village to another, proclaiming the good news of the kingdom of God. The Twelve were with him, and also some women who had been cured of evil spirits and diseases: Mary (called Magdalene) from whom seven demons had come out; Joanna the wife of Chuza, the manager of Herod's household; Susanna; and many others. These women were helping to support them out of their own means.

Not only do we learn that these women are supporting Jesus's ministry financially, but Luke mentions several of them by name. These women, along with the larger group of unnamed women are "with Jesus" like the Twelve are. With the exception of Peter, the Twelve serve mostly as "undifferentiated appendages." However these named women above are notable exceptions to that trend. This scene foreshadows future events in Luke-Acts. First, the sharing of possessions modeled by these women is an example

---

6. See ch. 8, "The Final Week," and the section there entitled "The Mechanisms of Betrayal."

7. Matthew 27:3–10 is the only Gospel account of Judas' death. Luke records it in Acts 1:18–19. There are numerous other places where Luke intentionally avoids dealing with an issue in Luke because he plans to deal with it more fully in Acts. See Fox, "Storytelling Sequels."

8. Brown, *Gospels as Stories*, 52–62.

of something that will become more pronounced in Acts, when the early Christians live together and share possessions.[9] More importantly, though, it will be the women, Joanna and Mary specifically mentioned by name, who will witness and testify to the resurrection of Jesus.

Luke also mentions that Joanna is married to the manager of Herod's household. This would connect her with significant wealth but would also make her something of a controversial figure, like Levi the tax collector, although in a different way.[10] For Luke this is part of his intentional presentation of Jesus and his influence; God's invitation is to all, regardless of previous life or political connections.

We also see the faithful and foil contrast play out in the story of Mary and Martha. In Luke 10:38–42, Martha opens her home to Jesus and makes herself busy with the preparations of hospitality—the picture of faithfully honoring a guest in the ancient world. Mary, by contrast, sits passively and listens to Jesus teach, something that exasperates Martha, who urges Jesus to involve himself in the dispute. While Martha is concerned with honoring Jesus through hospitality, Mary has recognized the words of the Lord, the prophet, and what she has chosen is better. Still, despite Jesus's praise of Mary, his critique of Martha is not a strong one, and certainly less than that of Simon in 7:36–50.[11] While Martha represents faithful hospitality, Mary is a foil to those expectations. In a scene of reversal, Jesus praises what is a cultural faux pas in favor of listening and learning. This is also an interesting scene of Jesus praising a female disciple who foregoes the cultural expectations in order to honor and follow Jesus.

The most significant role the women play, however, will be at the resurrection of Jesus. While the women are specifically introduced in chapter 8, they are mostly in the background for the rest of the Galilean ministry and the journey to Jerusalem. However, they are present at the crucifixion (23:49), with Luke specifically noting that they followed him from Galilee. What is more, an angel will say to the women, "He is not here; he has risen! Remember how he told you, while he was still with you in Galilee: 'The Son of Man must be delivered over to the hands of sinners, be crucified and on the third day be raised again.' Then they remembered his words" (24:6–8).

---

9. Acts 1:13–14; 2:41–47, as Johnson points out (*Gospel of Luke*, 134).

10. Parsons, *Luke*, 133. See also the connection to Herod in Acts 13:1. Whereas Levi, like Zacchaeus, seems complicit in his dishonest dealings, Joanna is merely associated by marriage with an enemy in the story.

11. Parsons points out the rhetorical device of *conduplication* used to indicate compassion or pity (*Luke*, 182–83).

Thus, it is revealed that these women were included in the disciples all along, even when they were not specifically mentioned.[12] Women will continue to be important for Luke in Acts, including Lydia (Acts 16:14–15), Priscilla (18:2–26), and the daughters of Phillip (21:9).

OTHER COMPANIONS

As we bring this chapter to a close, a few other groups of companions deserve mention. While we have discussed the Twelve and the women, there is a larger, less clear group of the disciples. We may see this group most clearly in the group of seventy-two sent by Jesus in Luke 10:1–24. This follows the scene at the beginning of chapter 9 where Jesus sends out the Twelve (9:1–6), so it seems clear that these seventy-two are separate from the Twelve, since the narrator declares these as seventy-two "others." Jesus gives them significant instructions as he sends them out, and they return with joy, as "even the demons submit to us in your name." This group of seventy-two, though not specifically numbered as such again, represent the larger group of disciples, and though they are "undifferentiated appendages," they represent the faithful who follow Jesus.[13]

Similarly, the crowds, also sometimes called the people, play a role as undifferentiated appendages as well. The crowds, also representative of John the Baptist's ministry, are at times recipients of compassion and healing (5:15; 9:11) or of rebuke and challenge (3:7; 11:29), or witnesses to his ministry (7:9–12, 24; 11:14), or even an obstacle to his safety (4:30; 8:42). By the time Jesus comes to Jerusalem for the last week of his life, the crowds are the reason the authorities are unable to arrest him because they hang on his words.

Thus, Jesus has a number of companions in Luke who play different roles at different times. Each of these roles allows Luke to flesh the narrative out more and fully present the hero, Jesus. We will now shift in our

---

12. Brown uses this as an example of analepsis, where the reader finds out at the end that these women were present all along (*Luke*, 182–83).

13. We may see contrasted with this the statement about Jesus's mother and brothers in 8:19–21. Luke describes a scene where Jesus's family members have trouble getting to him because of the crowds. When Jesus is notified, he responds by saying, "My mother and brothers are those who hear God's word and put it into practice." Commentators differ on whether Jesus is redefining who his family is based on obedience (Bock, *Luke*, 1:748; as in Mark 3:20–35) or if he is stating that it is specifically his mother and brothers who do the will of God (Parsons, *Luke*, 137; Johnson, *Gospel of Luke*, 133).

PART 2: INITIATION

examination of the hero to one of the most famous stages in any hero story, the road of trials.

DISCUSSION QUESTIONS

1. Who are your favorite companion characters in movies and books?
2. Which of the companions of Jesus in Luke do you find the most interesting?
3. Who have been the people in your life who have played significant roles as faithful companions?

6

The Road of Trials

Once having traversed the threshold, the hero moves in a dream landscape of curiously fluid, ambiguous forms, where he must survive a succession of trials. This is a favorite phase of the myth-adventure. It has produced a world literature of miraculous tests and ordeals. The hero is covertly aided by the advice, amulets, and secret agents of the supernatural helper whom he met before his entrance into this region. Or it may be that he here discovers for the first time that there is a benign power everywhere supporting him in his superhuman passage.
—Joseph Campbell, *The Hero with a Thousand Faces*, 97

Jesus returned to Galilee powerful in the Spirit. News that he was back spread through the countryside. He taught in their meeting places to everyone's acclaim and pleasure.
—Luke 4:14–15 MSG

THE ROAD OF TRIALS may be the longest and most iconic stage of the Hero's Journey. We can easily imagine scenes of Superman battling mad super criminals, Batman expunging the darkness from Gotham City, or Neo battling agents while plugged into the Matrix. Indeed, entire movies filled with action sequences sometimes make up the road of trials for a hero. If one imagines the three simplest stages of a heroic arc as the birth and introduction to the hero, fighting crime, and the final battle—the middle category representing the road of trials—we can imagine that three-part narrative being told in a single novel or movie or being spread out over a trilogy. *The Matrix* and the original *Star Wars* trilogy are excellent examples of trilogies that follow this template.

For Jesus, we can observe a road of trials starting with the first days of his public ministry all the way to just before his entrance into Jerusalem for the final week of his life. This covers more than fourteen chapters of content, all fleshing out the character of Jesus in Luke and building toward the climax. We will view this road of trials for Jesus in two larger sections. First, this chapter covers the Galilean ministry where Jesus makes himself known to the people in Galilee and establishes his identity. The next chapter will look more specifically at Jesus's journey to Jerusalem, a key narrative and directional shift in Luke. While we may be tempted to think this break in the narrative between the Galilean ministry and the road to Jerusalem is arbitrary, these two phases of Jesus's ministry in Luke have very unique features and emotional tones. During the Galilean ministry, an emphasis will be placed on Jesus being the Son of God, powerful in word and deed. People will regularly be amazed and astonished by what he says and does, and more than a few people he encounters will fall at his feet. Luke wants you to form an opinion early on about the significance of Jesus in this world. While the story of Jesus is leading to a tragic and violent collision with the powers, that is not on display yet from these early scenes, as it builds towards an epiphany on the Mount of Transfiguration. By contrast, the travel narrative is different, with more teaching and more escalating conflict with the religious leaders. We will discuss the travel narrative in the next chapter.

RELEASING THOSE IN BONDAGE

Immediately following the crossing of the threshold scene in Nazareth, Jesus goes to the Capernaum synagogue.[1] While teaching in the synagogue, Jesus encounters a man with an unclean spirit and casts it out of him. This

---

1. Most commentators see the Galilean ministry officially starting in 4:14; here we see that first scene in Nazareth as Jesus crossing the threshold.

The Road of Trials

scene is emblematic of so many of the scenes in the road of trials for Jesus, and we do well to notice them here at the start. We tend to focus on the miraculous, the dramatic elements in stories like this, but Luke is careful to tell us that this miracle happens in the context of Jesus teaching. The people "were amazed" at his teaching because "his words had authority" (Luke 4:32).

The first trial for our hero is encountering demonic forces.[2] While Jesus is teaching, a man with a demon cries out, recognizing him as "the Holy One of God" (4:34). It stands as high irony throughout Luke-Acts that while the religious leaders continually question and doubt Jesus's identity, the demons immediately recognize and declare him as the Messiah.[3] Jesus being in the power of the Spirit (4:14) is the radical opposite of this unclean spirit. Rising to the occasion, Jesus rebukes the unclean spirit, and it obeys him; the demon leaves, and the man is uninjured (4:35). As foreshadowed in the Nazareth sermon that quoted Isa 61, Jesus is releasing those who are in bondage.

Two key elements surface here. First, Luke demonstrates that Jesus is powerful in word and in deed. Being powerful in word (λογός) is a key element for Luke's hero. It was a concept introduced in the prologue (1:2) and continues throughout Luke-Acts.[4] Jesus teaches with power and authority; the demons as well as the forces of nature—the wind and the waves—listen to him. Indeed, Jesus is powerful in word. These powerful words are combined with powerful actions—exorcisms, healings, and other miracles. The travelers on the road to Emmaus will later describe Jesus as "a prophet, powerful in word and deed before God and all the people" (24:19). Stephen will likewise proclaim Moses as powerful in word and deed (7:22), and numerous figures in Acts will embody this twofold description as well (Peter, Stephen, Philip, Paul).[5] Jesus first demonstrates that quality of the prophetic

---

2. We might see the first trial as his encountering the crowd in Nazareth or even as his showdown with Satan in the wilderness. While the Hero's Journey works as a helpful template to analyze Luke-Acts, we need not split hairs or overly force the narrative into the template, or vice versa. As such, don't put too much emphasis on what we count as Jesus's first trial.

3. For the religious leaders doubting or questioning Jesus, see Luke 5:21, 30, 33; 6:2; 11:53; 15:2; 19:39. For a list of demons declaring his identity, see Luke 4:3, 9, 34, 41; 8:28.

4. Luke 4:32; 5:1; 8:11, 21; 11:28; Acts 4:4; 6:2, 7; 8:4; 19:10.

5. Stephen's speech also specifically includes a reference to Deut 18:15, which speaks of God raising up a prophet like Moses. For more on the specific similarities between Moses and Jesus in Luke, see Fox, *Hermeneutics of Social Identity*, 123–27.

task here through authoritative teaching and casting out demons. These marvelous words and deeds "reveal the essence of Jesus' character."[6]

Second, we notice how the people are amazed. This will be a common occurrence in Luke, specifically in the birth narratives and in the Galilean ministry: people are regularly amazed at Jesus. In the birth narratives, amazement came from different sources, such as angels, or the reports from the shepherds, or the naming of John the Baptist. In the Galilean ministry, people are specifically amazed by Jesus—his teaching and his deeds.

Luke will use a handful of different words to communicate this idea. While these words are not all equivalent to one another, the reader can see their connection in the way the people respond to Jesus. Luke uses three different root words that get translated as "amaze" in English to describe people's reaction to Jesus.[7] He will also use "marvel" and "awe."[8] Sometimes these will be paired together, for example, in 5:26 where Luke reports, "Everyone was amazed and gave praise to God. They were filled with awe and said, 'We have seen remarkable things today.'" Luke is concerned to demonstrate the remarkable ministry of Jesus and the people's response to it.[9]

Following the experience in the synagogue, Jesus goes to the house of Simon and, after healing Simon's mother-in-law, encounters numerous people with sicknesses and diseases, healing them and casting out demons (4:38–44). This is the next trial for our hero: sickness. As before, the demons recognize him as the Messiah, and he again does not allow them to speak (4:41). Jesus then retreats to a solitary (i.e., wilderness) place. The people try to keep him from leaving, but he asserts he must proclaim the kingdom of God to other towns.[10] We notice the stark contrast between the crowd in Nazareth with their intense anger compared to Capernaum, where they want Jesus to stay, thus validating Jesus's statement that "no prophet is accepted in his hometown" (4:24).

---

6. Parsons, *Luke*, 86.
7. The Greek words used are ἔκστασις, ἐκπλήσσω, and ἐξίστημι.
8. The Greek words used are θαυμάζω and φόβος.
9. Luke 4:22, 32; 5:26; 8:25, 35, 56; 7:16; 9:43.
10. The narrator's statement that ends that section—that Jesus kept preaching in the synagogues of Judea—is puzzling, since Jesus just left Capernaum and is next headed to the Sea of Galilee, both in Galilee, not Judea.

The Road of Trials

PROPHETIC CRITIQUE

After the formal introduction of Simon and calling the first disciples, covered in chapter 5, Jesus goes to an unnamed town and has the first of several encounters that challenge the religious status quo. The next five scenes will all present Jesus as an iconoclastic figure in the context of first-century Judaism. This is a key part of Jesus's prophetic task; as he proclaims the good news to the oppressed and releases those in bondage, he necessarily critiques the elements of the systems of his day. As the prophets before him brought a challenging message and were rejected—even as recently seen in the narrative with John the Baptist—so Jesus will bring a challenging message in his day.

The first scene is Jesus's encounter with a leper. The man, like several others in the road of trials, falls humbly before Jesus with his face on the ground, begging, "If you are willing, you can make me clean." Jesus touches the man, saying, "I am willing. Be clean" (5:13). The man is immediately healed, and Jesus instructs him to show himself to the priest and take the necessary steps from Lev 13–14.

Matthew Thiessen rightly corrects a misconception that is widespread and pervasive; the condition discussed in the Gospels (Gk: *lepra*), in Leviticus (Heb: *tsara'at*), and numerous other places in the Old and New Testaments, is not the disease we think of today (Hanson's disease, colloquially called leprosy) that causes numbness in the extremities and the loss of limbs but, rather, is a relatively minor skin condition that resulted in ritual impurity.[11] This minor skin condition, while not sinful, came with significant social consequences, which might have included expulsion from the community (Lev 13:45–46).[12] In healing the man, Jesus allows him to be restored to his community and a more normal way of life. While Jesus does not seem to fully eliminate the system of ritual purity, he also does not fully adhere to it, instead taking a middle road of prophetic challenge. Jesus challenges social conventions by touching the man in the process of healing him, an act that would make him unclean (Lev 22:4–6).[13] That said, he also

---

11. Thiessen, *Jesus and the Forces*, 43–54.

12. While Jesus encounters him in a town, we might wonder the degree to which the practices from Leviticus were being followed.

13. Also confirmed in practice at Qumran, 4Q396 III, 4–11; and in Josephus *Ant.* 3.11.3 §264. See Parsons, *Luke*, 90. It is obvious that Jesus could have healed the man without touching him, as he does in Luke 17:11–19, healing ten lepers only by giving them a command. Jesus's action of touching the leper here seems intentional, as

PART 2: INITIATION

tells the man to present himself to the priest and go through the proper steps required in the law, thus not totally abrogating the ritual purity system. Indeed, Jesus was firmly within the Judaism of the first century, while at the same time, his role as a prophet led him to challenge and disrupt the status quo as it stood.[14] Green puts it well, saying, "Jesus is presented as one who is both able and willing to cross conventional boundaries to bring good news. On the other hand, his practices are in harmony with Moses."[15] As we will see, Jesus does similar things with regard to fasting, the Sabbath, and handwashing rituals. The difference here is that he receives no criticism from the teachers of the law, as they appear not to be present. Rather than the ritual impurity extending to Jesus by touching the man (Lev 22:4–6), Jesus, who is in the power of the Holy Spirit, heals the man. With Jesus, the process works in reverse.[16]

---

evidenced by the following scenes that also similarly challenge the status quo. Thiessen is adamant here that rather than opposing the Jewish ritual purity system, Jesus works within it, as all Jews of the first century did (*Jesus and the Forces*, 55). He also asserts that touching a person with this condition is not sinful, but rather, "one only needs to be careful neither to transmit that impurity into sacred space nor to handle sacred vessels of food" (62). While his larger critique is valid and needed due to a misunderstanding of *lepra* by modern Christians, he underemphasizes the social impact this disease had in the first century. Despite his mention of Lev 13:45–46 about a person with this skin condition living outside of the camp—certainly a debilitating social arrangement, removed from family, public religious practice, and some forms of social engagement—and that it is equated with death in numerous places in the OT (Num 12:12; 2 Kgs 5:7), Thiessen's summary of the condition overly minimizes these social restrictions. He also overlooks the daring move Jesus makes by touching the man with this condition (mentioning it on p. 65 but not discussing the significance). While we also must seek to have an accurate view of Jewish ritual purity in the first century—it was not particularly arduous to Jewish people—leprosy seems to have been among the more severe social conditions. For more on ritual purity in first-century Judaism, see Brown and Roberts, "Reading Judaism Ethically"; Levine, "Discharging Responsibility."

14. This position puts me at odds with scholars like Matthew Thiessen, Paula Fredriksen, and others, who argue that Jesus was fully in line with the Judaism of his day and any attempt to see him deviating from that Judaism is a later Christian addition. While I concur that we need to understand Jesus as operating within the context of first-century Judaism, we must also understand his key role as a prophet, as all the Gospels writers, but Luke-Acts specifically, do. And while we should be careful to avoid the later false alternative of Judaism equals legalism, while Christianity equals grace, that should not lead us to conclude that Jesus or other prophetic figures in the New Testament, like John the Baptist, Peter, Paul, etc., would not or could not have critiqued the Judaism of their day. See Fredriksen, "Did Jesus Oppose?"; Fredriken, "What You See."

15. Green, *Gospel of Luke*, 237–38.

16. In addition, part of Jesus's prophetic, messianic ministry is healing lepers, like

The Road of Trials

Despite Jesus's orders not to tell anyone, the word about Jesus spreads; this is a minor literary irony for Luke in that the more Jesus tries to keep his presence and identity a secret, the more word about him spreads and the crowds seek him out. Again Jesus withdraws to a wilderness place to pray (5:16).

The popularity continues in the next scene as Jesus is teaching in a house where people had come from "every village of Galilee and from Judea and Jerusalem" (5:17a). The narrator tells us that "the power of the Lord was on Jesus to heal the sick" (5:17b). Unable to get to Jesus because of the crowd, they remove tiles from the roof to lower the man down before Jesus (5:19).[17] We can appreciate the daring nature of this move by the friends. Jesus can, too, as when he sees *their* faith—either the friends or all of the men, including the paralytic—he says to the man, "Friend, your sins are forgiven" (5:20).

For the second story in a row, Jesus challenges Jewish convention, as the Pharisees and teachers of the law think to themselves that he is committing blasphemy, doing what only God can do, namely, forgive sins. Knowing their thoughts, Jesus challenges them: "Which is easier: to say, 'Your sins are forgiven,' or to say, 'Get up and walk'? But I want you to know that the Son of Man has authority on earth to forgive sins.' So he said to the paralyzed man, 'I tell you, get up, take your mat and go home'" (5:23–24). If there was any doubt about the authority of Jesus, or his ability to forgive sins, or suspicion that he may talk a good game but is unable to back it up with his actions, Luke removes all doubt. The man is healed immediately and walks home, carrying his bed (5:25).

Here we encounter our next force of opposition that will recur on the road of trials: the religious leaders. This conflict continues in the following story, where Jesus encounters Levi at his tax booth. Tax collectors are considered a particularly heinous group in the Gospels, Jews who work for Rome getting wealthy by overtaxing their fellow countrymen.[18] They were not liked and particularly not by the Pharisees, who doubled down on holy living and derided those who didn't. Not only does Jesus call Levi to follow

---

Moses (Num 12); Elijah (2 Kgs 5); and later references to John's disciples (7:22) (Thiessen, *Jesus and the Forces*, 62–63).

17. While there are similar accounts of this story in both Matthew (9:2–8) and Mark (2:3–12), Matthew eliminates the details of the house and the crowd, and Mark uses intensified language, saying the friends were "digging" in the roof. Parsons attributes this to Luke contextualizing for his more urban, Mediterranean audience (*Luke*, 90–91).

18. See Downs, "Economics," 224–25.

him, but he attends a banquet at Levi's house with a large crowd of tax collectors, attracting the critical eye of the "Pharisees and teachers of the law." In Luke-Acts, Jesus will take criticism as an opportunity to clarify his mission.[19] We again see Jesus critique the Jewish status quo, demonstrating his mission of inclusion, a feature of Luke that will extend for two volumes.

This then leads to those same religious leaders questioning him about fasting. Once again, Jesus does not reject the Jewish system of fasting, for he and his disciples will fast (Luke 4:1–2; Acts 13:2; 14:23; 27:9). But the presence of Jesus, the Son of God, is a time for feasting, not fasting.[20] He then tells them a parable about garments and patches, wine and wineskins, drawing a distinct line between the old and the new. Scholars debate whether readers should understand Jesus equating his ways with the old or with the new in this parable.[21] However, we should not let that distract us from the main point; Jesus is making a statement about his teachings and mission as a prophetic critique against the status quo of the Pharisees and teachers of the law, which we now see played out in the fourth episode in a row, namely, ritual purity, forgiveness, table fellowship, and fasting.

This is immediately followed by a fifth story of critique, specifically regarding the Sabbath. More accurately stated, Luke 6:1–11 includes two stories about the Sabbath together. In the first, while walking through a field, Jesus's disciples pick some heads of grain to eat and are accused by Pharisees of breaking the Sabbath. Jesus appeals to David and ends by stating, "The Son of man is Lord of the Sabbath" (6:5). This is then followed by another Sabbath story of Jesus teaching in a synagogue and encounters a man with a shriveled hand. While the opponents are watching him and trying to accuse him, Jesus has the man stand up in front of everyone (6:8). "Then Jesus said to them, 'I ask you, which is lawful on the Sabbath: to

---

19. This is the first of a type scene that I call the critic response type scene, also in Luke 15:1–32; 19:1–10; Acts 11:1–18. See Fox, *Hermeneutics of Social Identity*, 78–86.

20. Parsons, *Luke*, 94; Green, *Gospel of Luke*, 249.

21. Traditionally it was viewed that the way of the Pharisees and the teachers of the law was the old way, with Jesus representing the new. For this view, see Fitzmyer, *Luke I–IX*, 594–97; Bock, *Luke*, 1:518–22; Nolland, *Luke 1:1—9:20*, 250–51; Johnson, *Gospel of Luke*, 99. More recently, some scholars have opted to see Jesus, as represented by his birth narrative, genealogy, temptation, and sermon in Nazareth, representing the ancient purpose of God, rooted in Jewish antiquity. This is also supported by the next two stories regarding the Sabbath, appealing to the old, the law, as justification. This is a compelling take, but the evidence is too finely balanced to judge with certainty, especially with v. 39. For this view, see Green, *Gospel of Luke*, 237–38; and Parsons, *Luke*, 95–96, who has a good discussion of this understanding.

do good or to do evil, to save life or to destroy it?'" Jesus heals the man, making the Pharisees and teachers of the law furious (6:11). This is the first of several times in Luke that Jesus heals on the Sabbath.[22] We understand this as a continuation of the leitmotif we have seen of Jesus challenging the status quo. He does not desire to abolish Sabbath observance; rather, he desires to challenge the practice of Sabbath in this time, namely, regulations that prohibited doing something good, and instead restore the Sabbath as a life-giving tradition, a time to restore and to do good.

JESUS'S TEACHING

While the Galilean ministry is largely made up of the prophetic actions of Jesus, Luke does not fail to include some teaching sections. The Sermon on the Plain (6:17–49) is the longest section of teaching by Jesus in the Galilean ministry. In addition to noting the large crowd from faraway regions, the same elements of his prophetic role are emphasized; he teaches the word of God, works wonders, and is identified with power.[23]

His teaching also continues to further the prophetic critique that comes with his message and kingdom. The blessed in Jesus's world are the poor, the hungry, those who weep, and those who are hated and insulted. By contrast, Jesus pronounces woes to the rich, the well fed, those who laugh now, and those whom people speak well of (6:20–26). "Human society perpetuates structures of injustice and exclusion, but God intervenes on the side of the oppressed," Tannehill says. "The disruptive effect of this intervention is often presented in Luke as a reversal of the structures of society: those with power, status, and riches are put down and those without them are exalted."[24] These elements were introduced in the birth

---

22. I have written previously that Luke has five accounts of Jesus performing healings on the Sabbath (Fox, *Hermeneutics of Social Identity*, 73n138). This may be true if where Jesus drives out an impure spirit (4:31–37) and when, apparently on the same day before sundown, Jesus heals Simon's mother-in-law (4:38–40), are seen as Sabbath healings. However, they differ from the others in that he receives no criticism from his opponents for these. The others (6:6–11; 13:10–17; 14:1–6) are clear examples that the author identifies as Sabbath healings and should get the most of our attention in this regard.

23. While the phrases "word of God," "preach the gospel," and "Holy Spirit" are not specifically used here, Luke is obviously presenting a continuation of the prophetic ministry we have seen thus far from Jesus in the Galilean ministry.

24. Tannehill, *Gospel According to Luke*, 109.

PART 2: INITIATION

narratives,[25] and it is easy to see why this was not a popular message for the wealthy and those in power, whether religious or political.

Jesus continues his prophetic challenge by charging his audience to love their enemies (6:27, 35), perhaps the most difficult command in the teachings of our hero. In addition, however challenging this command seems to us—which is real and formidable—we must remember the context of first-century Roman occupation and oppression of this land by the Romans. Despite merely challenging his listeners to love the enemies in their midst, Luke shows Jesus modeling this love for his enemies. Several times as the tension between Jesus and his opponents escalates and reaches its climax, Jesus will extend love to his enemies, even to the very end.[26] Indeed, this hero practices what he preaches.

TWO STORIES

Chapter 7 begins with two healing stories, the centurion's slave and the widow's son. These two healings communicate important thematic and strategic storytelling elements that serve to bolster the two-volume narrative.

The story of the centurion stands out as particularly interesting. As mentioned, the regions of Galilee and Judea were under the control and occupation of Rome. This was largely an acrimonious relationship, due to taxation and violent subversion on Rome's part and rebellion on the Jewish side, but here we see a notable exception. This centurion in Capernaum is a friend and advocate of the local Jewish population. He built their synagogue and loves the Jewish people, as the Jewish elders of the town attest. This is a classic example of the rhetorical strategy of building an ethos for the character; before the centurion even speaks or engages with Jesus, the narrator has made sure the reader knows what to think of him. This is confirmed afterwards by Jesus's comments as well: "I tell you, I have not found such great faith even in Israel" (7:9). By his faith in Jesus's authority and trusting his word, the centurion works as a foil to the Pharisees and teachers of the law. While they "reject the purposes of God" (7:29–30), this centurion trusts Jesus's authority and seems to have special insight into his identity as God's Son and prophet. In addition, this has similarities to Elisha healing Naaman the Syrian, a foreign soldier whom Jesus referenced in 4:27.[27]

25. Luke 1:51–53; 2:34.
26. Luke 22:51; 23:34.
27. For a chart with the similarities between these stories made plain, see Green, *Gospel of Luke*, 284.

The Road of Trials

"Soon afterward" Jesus goes to the city of Nain, a city six miles southeast of Nazareth (7:11).[28] There are clear intertextual similarities to Elijah in 1 Kgs 17, a story also previously referenced by Jesus (4:26). However, even though Jesus shows similarities to Elijah in his prophetic ministry, Luke is careful to show how Jesus outdoes and improves upon the ministry of Elijah. Elijah is a valued and respected member of Jewish tradition; however, the kingdom of Jesus surpasses that of Elijah by including outsiders and expanding the mission beyond Jews. Jesus touches the bier (the slab the corpse is laying on), again "[crossing] the boundaries of ritual purity" for the purpose of healing.[29] The crowd responds, saying, "A great prophet has appeared among us . . . God has come to help his people" (7:16). Luke reaffirms Jesus's identity, insisting that God has not abandoned his people but is involved in this enchanted world.

These two stories of healing, pairing male and female recipients of Jesus's saving work, contribute to the larger two-volume narrative of Luke-Acts. Soldiers responding positively to the way of Jesus will happen again, both the conversion of Sergius Paulus by Paul (Acts 13:7) and, more importantly, the conversion of Cornelius the centurion by Peter (Acts 10). The conversion of this unnamed centurion in Luke 7 is a significant foreshadowing of the dramatic experience Peter has that results in the inclusion of gentiles in the family of God. The healing of the widow's son, as mentioned, serves to move the ministry of Jesus past the ministry of Elijah and the prophets in the Hebrew Scriptures to something more. Jesus is in the tradition of Elijah and at the same time eclipses Elijah in significant ways. While the seeds are planted here, this will be made more explicit as Jesus transitions from Galilean ministry to the journey to Jerusalem in chapter 9.

THE GUEST OF SIMON

Two more scenes need attention before we leave the Galilean ministry behind. In the first, Jesus goes to be the guest of Simon the Pharisee. This is the first of the Pharisees whom Luke names.[30] We must be careful to avoid

---

28. Green, *Gospel of Luke*, 290.
29. Green, *Gospel of Luke*, 292. As in 5:12–13.
30. Some see parallel stories in the three other Gospels (Matt 26:6–13; Mark 14:3–9; John 12:1–8; the parable from 7:41–42 is paralleled in Matt 18:23–24). Those Gospels have the scene occurring in Bethany just before Jesus enters Jerusalem for the last week of his life. Scholars disagree if this is the same or different story. For a deeper comparison, see Johnson, *Gospel of Luke*, 128–29.

any hasty generalization about Pharisees here. While thus far in Luke the Pharisees, along with the teachers of the law, are Jesus's philosophical opponents, we notice that they continue to engage with him and, here, show him hospitality and invite him to dinner. Green reminds us of two other points on this regard, first that a dichotomy between "the Pharisees" and "the people" is false, as over the course of Luke-Acts not all of "the people" or "the crowds" respond positively to Jesus and not all of the Pharisees respond poorly. Second, plenty of time remains for Luke to revise his presentation of the Pharisees, which he seems to do later in the narrative.[31] The Pharisees do remain an opponent for Jesus here, all while extending hospitality and spirited debate. This spirited debate allows for Luke to distinguish how Jesus's teaching and kingdom message are both similar to and different from the message of the Pharisees.

The sinful woman extravagantly demonstrates repentance and her love and gratitude for Jesus in her acts. Her sinful reputation prompts Simon to say, "If this man were a prophet, he would know who is touching him and what kind of woman she is—that she is a sinner" (Luke 7:39). We are again confronted with the question of prophecy, namely, Simon's view of what it means to be a prophet. For Simon, a prophet should be aware of the sinfulness of another and send her away. For Jesus, lived embodiment of the prophetic role means being a compassionate healer and forgiver of the sinful. This extension of forgiveness causes a stir among the guests, who ask, as was asked previously in 5:21, "Who is this that even forgives sins?" (7:49). Having seen Jesus forgive sins previously, to the shock of the religious leaders present, the reader is beginning to expect the prophetic actions of Jesus to spark controversy.

This meal scene, along with two others in Luke (11:37–54; 14:1–24), may be viewed as examples of the Hellenistic symposium.[32] In Greek literature, there were oftentimes scenes of shared meals that included a host, a chief guest who is given a special invitation, and other guests. The guest of honor is regularly revealed to have a particular wisdom that stands out over the others present. Conversation of a philosophical nature takes place after the meal, which often involves asking and answering questions. There is also regularly a moment in the scene that gives rise to the teaching or discission after the meal—in this case the actions of the woman. If this template is in view in these scenes in Luke, it shows us several things. First, it

---

31. Green, *Gospel of Luke*, 302–3.
32. Steele, "Luke 11:37–54."

The Road of Trials

shows how Luke is intentional in using the literary conventions of his day. Taking a page from Plato and Xenophon, Luke seeks to communicate the story of Jesus in a way his readers will engage with and understand. Second, we might view Jesus's teaching after the meal as a particular kind of wisdom Jesus represents. As Socrates had his particular kind of wisdom, so Jesus has his. Jesus is notably different than other philosophical teachers in that he specifically focuses on forgiving and welcoming repentant sinners.

THE EPIPHANY

Last, we need to talk about the climactic scene of the Galilean ministry, the transfiguration. In hero stories, there is often a significant event at the end of the road of trials, an epiphany that changes the worldview of the hero in some way and sets the course for the next stage of the adventure. In *Star Wars: A New Hope*, Luke Skywalker realizes that Princess Leia is a prisoner on the Death Star and is scheduled for execution.[33] In *The Matrix*, Neo understands that the Oracle was right and realizes he has to try to save Morpheus.[34] In Luke, the transfiguration occurs at the midway point of the road of trials, right before the transition from the Galilean ministry to the journey to Jerusalem.[35] Jesus has arrived on the scene in the power of the Holy Spirit, he has declared the good news of God, and he has performed signs and wonders. There is one primary thing left to do, and it needs to happen in Jerusalem, for "no prophet can die outside of Jerusalem" (Luke 13:33).

The transfiguration scene is preceded by two others, and Luke is very intentional in tying these together. Jesus, praying with his disciples, asks them who the crowds say he is (9:18). After various responses, Jesus asks them, "Who do you say I am?" Peter responds, "God's Messiah" (9:20). Jesus strictly warns them not to tell anyone, before he predicts his rejection, death, and resurrection. He then talks about the cost of being a disciple, saying that it requires one to "take up their cross daily" (9:23). It is clear that these scenes—Peter's confession, the cost of being Jesus's disciple, and the

---

33. Lucas, *New Hope*. See also Soloponte, *Ultimate Hero's Journey*, 119.

34. Wachowskis, *Matrix*. Soloponte, *Ultimate Hero's Journey*, 119.

35. Campbell sees the transfiguration as part of the stage of master of two worlds but sees the use of epiphany language as more significant to the disciples—in the call to abandon their attachments and lose their loves—than to Jesus (*Hero with Thousand Faces*, 236–37).

PART 2: INITIATION

transfiguration are connected. "Taken together," Johnson says, "they lead the disciples (and the reader) into a deeper understanding of Jesus' identity and their call."[36] This has been the primary goal of the Galilean ministry, and we now see it capped off in a significant way.

Jesus takes three disciples with him up a mountain to pray.[37] There are several elements the reader should notice from this scene. First, we are right to notice connections with Jesus's baptism by John back in 3:21–22. Despite the significant elements in the baptism—the Holy Spirit descending as a dove and the voice from heaven—it is a rather short scene. The transfiguration is a richer and more densely symbolic scene. In the same way the baptism of Jesus inaugurated the Galilean ministry and set the course for what was to follow, namely, the road of trials and Jesus demonstrating his identity as the true Son of God and prophet like Moses, the transfiguration inaugurates the journey to Jerusalem and likewise sets the stage for what is to come at the end of the journey, the ordeal.

Second, Luke mentions that Jesus is speaking with two Old Testament figures, Moses and Elijah, and tells the reader that they were talking about "his exodus" (τὴν ἔξοδον αὐτοῦ), which he was about to bring to fulfillment in Jerusalem (9:31).[38] This is a clear transition point in the direction of the narrative, looking ahead to the journey about to commence. In addition, it is also an intentional signifier that Jesus, like Moses before him, is leading an exodus. What Luke has strongly hinted at previously, he now makes explicit: Jesus is the prophet like Moses who leads people in a new exodus out of the slavery of sin. The heavenly voice directly matches the wording in Deut 18:15: *Listen to him*.[39] Additionally, Moses and Elijah were both prophets who were thought to have ascended into heaven in remarkable ways, Moses on the mountain and Elijah in the fiery chariot.[40] Jesus, too, will have his own ascension moment at the end of Luke and the beginning of Acts. Last, both Moses and Elijah appointed successors, Joshua and Elisha, who acted in the Spirit.[41] Jesus promises the Spirit to his followers

---

36. Johnson, *Gospel of Luke*, 154.

37. Bock notes that when prayer is present in Luke, "something significant usually follows" (*Luke*, 1:866).

38. Neither Mark nor Matthew includes this detail. Many commentators discuss the significance of these two characters. For a good summary of the views, see Bock, *Luke*, 1:868–69.

39. Bock, *Luke*, 1:874. See Deut 18:15 LXX.

40. Deut 34; 2 Kgs 2. See Johnson, *Gospel of Luke*, 164.

41. Num 27:12–23; 2 Kgs 2. Johnson, *Gospel of Luke*, 164.

(Luke 24:49), and they will continue his ministry as well. For all of these reasons, Moses and Elijah are great precursors to the prophetic ministry of Jesus.

Luke also emphasizes Jesus's glory.[42] In the previous scene discussing the cost of being his disciple, Jesus mentioned the Son of Man coming in the glory of his Father, including the note that some would not taste death before they see the kingdom of God. They now see his glory revealed. This reference to glory looks forward to the culmination of Jesus's ministry, after the suffering, the ordeal, to his resurrection. Jesus will later say to the travelers on the road to Emmaus, "Did not the Messiah have to suffer these things and then enter his glory?" (24:26). This pattern of suffering followed by glory begins to take center stage.[43]

Two scenes end the Galilean ministry, continuing common themes we have seen. Jesus heals a boy who has a demon, which again causes amazement (9:37–43a). This leads Jesus to again predict his death and share about the upside-down nature of his kingdom (9:43b–54); the least among his followers is the greatest (9:46–48). Similarly, Jesus the Son of God will suffer the most on the way to glory.

What was merely hinted at before now comes into central focus: Jesus must go to Jerusalem to bring his mission to fulfillment. Jesus has proven his identity as the Son of God and prophet; God has confirmed this to him, and his closest followers have been witnesses of his ministry. Now the journey can begin. Indeed, when the narrative changes to traveling to Jerusalem, his ensuing arrest by the authorities and death become more and more in focus. Also heightened is the prophetic critique Jesus brings against the powers.

It is to that journey we now turn.

DISCUSSION QUESTIONS

1. Which scene from the Galilean ministry of Jesus is your favorite?

---

42. Neither Mark nor Matthew uses the word "glory." Luke has also expanded the scene to be longer than the other Synoptic Gospels.

43. It may be possible to connect the transfiguration to the stage in the Hero's Journey called meeting the goddess, or *magna mater*, which is when the hero meets a divine mother figure for encouragement and clarity. See Campbell, *Hero with a Thousand Faces*, 109–20; Soloponte, *Ultimate Hero's Journey*, i. I feel using the language and imagery of epiphany fits better with the transfiguration, so I have chosen to use it here.

2. Can you think of other epiphany scenes from books and movies that are significant?

3. Can you think of an experience in your own life that worked like an epiphany for you, clarifying and setting the stage for the journey you were going to take next?

7

The Journey

The original departure into the land of trials represented only the beginning of the long and really perilous path of initiatory conquests and moments of illumination. Dragons have to be slayed and surprising barriers passed—again, again, and again. Meanwhile there will be a multitude of preliminary victories, unretainable ecstasies, and momentary glimpses of the wonderful land.

—Joseph Campbell, *The Hero with a Thousand Faces*, 109

When it came close to the time for his Ascension, he gathered up his courage and steeled himself for the journey to Jerusalem.

—Luke 9:51 MSG

AFTER HAVING THE EPIPHANY experience on the Mount of Transfiguration, we encounter one of the most programmatic scenes in the narrative. As Luke will do in early Acts with Jesus saying that his disciples will be his witnesses in Jerusalem, Judea, Samaria, and the ends of the earth (Acts 1:8), which becomes something of a road map for the rest of Acts, Luke now tells his reader, "As the time approached for him to be taken up to heaven, Jesus resolutely set out for Jerusalem" (Luke 9:51). With the Galilean ministry

Part 2: Initiation

having established Jesus as the true Son of God and the prophet who embodies the Holy Spirit, announces good news, and performs signs and wonders, the focus of the narrative will now switch to Jerusalem. This passage introduces a theme that will play several important literary functions for Luke in his narrative:

First, as just mentioned, it sets the narrative course for the middle section of Luke's Gospel. Luke-Acts is geographically arranged, and we see that focus on display here. From 9:51 until right before Jesus enters the city (19:28), the narrative will be focused on his journey to Jerusalem. Jesus will have numerous encounters with people and crowds of people while on this journey. However, Luke does not let his reader forget that they are en route to the city. Sometimes this will be in a parenthetic remark (9:53; 13:22; 17:11; 18:31; 19:11), and other times Jerusalem will be a setting in the teaching of Jesus (10:30; 13:4, 33–34).[1]

Second, despite the ominous tone around Jerusalem as the place of the ordeal—the place Jesus will be arrested and killed, which Luke has told the reader several times—Jerusalem becomes a central geographical focus of Luke's two-volume narrative. Extending into Acts, where the ministry of the disciples starts and remains for the first seven chapters, more than twenty chapters of material in the narrative are set squarely in Jerusalem or in a conspicuous journey toward Jerusalem. Thus, in Luke we see something of a magnetic pull of Jesus and the disciples to the city for the climax; conversely, in Acts, Jerusalem will be the epicenter of the move of God that will move outward over the course of the rest of the narrative.[2]

Last, the journey to Jerusalem builds tension for the climax. As Jesus predicted in 9:21, the Son of Man must suffer, be rejected, die, and be raised to life. Jesus discusses with Moses and Elijah on the Mount of Transfiguration his exodus, which he is about to bring to fulfillment in Jerusalem. He predicts his being "delivered into the hands of men" again in 9:44, and even though the disciples don't understand this, the reader does. We know *how* this story ends. We know *where* the climax takes place. Lest we forget, Luke is careful to remind his reader regularly about Jesus's rejection, death, and resurrection (12:49–50; 13:33–34; 16:31; 17:25; 18:31–33; 19:14).[3] But we

---

1. Other places, Luke simply mentions that Jesus is "on the way," though he does not specifically mention Jerusalem, as in 9:52, 56, 57; 10:38; 13:33.

2. Blomberg has an effective illustration of this, showing the "hourglass" shape of the Luke-Acts narrative (*Jesus and the Gospels*, 162).

3. Tannehill, *Gospel According to Luke*, 229.

The Journey

need the hero in the right setting for his date with destiny. The journey to Jerusalem gets him there.

But the journey does more than that. While Luke has established Jesus as the prophet like Moses, he has certainly not closed the book on revealing to his reader who Jesus is. It is no coincidence that at the climactic moment at the end of the Galilean journey, the voice from heaven says, "This is my Son, whom I have chosen; *listen to him*" (9:35). This is intentional plotting and pacing, because a key emphasis during the journey to Jerusalem is Jesus's teaching. While Jesus will still perform miracles, a few of which are key to the narrative, miracles are less of a focus during this time. In addition, the heavenly voice's command to listen (or hear) will be reinforced in strategic places. In talking to his disciples in 10:23-24, Jesus talks of how kings and prophets wanted to see and hear what the disciples do but did not get to, and that whoever listens to them, listens to him (10:16). Jesus will also occasionally punctuate a teaching with a statement on hearing, such as "Blessed are those who hear " (11:28) or "Whoever has ears to hear let them hear" (14:35). And Luke also tells us that tax collectors and sinners "were all gathering around to hear Jesus" (15:1), as Mary does sitting at his feet (10:39), contrasted with the Pharisees and teachers of the law, who appear more on the fringes and sneer (16:14).

The teaching sections of the journey narrative will fall into four primary headings, which we will discuss individually.[4] But before we focus on Jesus's teaching ministry, we must first look at the scene that begins the journey to Jerusalem.

COMMENCING THE JOURNEY

Luke 9:51 tells us that Jesus resolutely sets out for Jerusalem (Gk: αὐτὸς τὸ πρόσωπον ἐστήρισεν τοῦ πορεύεσθαι εἰς Ἰερουσαλήμ [he set his face to go]). In the next line, movement is already taking place, as messengers go

---

4. I see four thematic categories: cost of discipleship, conflict, judgment and the apocalyptic, and kingdom teaching. Parsons sees three categories: life eternal, reversal, and the character of God (*Luke*, 163–65). Johnson views it more as having three different groups Jesus is speaking to, i.e., disciples, crowds, and opponents (i.e., Pharisees and teachers of the law) (*Gospel of Luke*, 164–65). Suffice it to say, this section of Luke can be difficult to neatly organize (Johnson, *Gospel of Luke*, 163; Brown, *Gospels as Stories*, xi–xii). While I think my four categories have merit, you as a careful reader should both balance my thoughts with those of other readers and (more importantly) see what emphases you notice in this section of teachings.

PART 2: INITIATION

ahead to a Samaritan village, where they are not welcomed because they are heading for Jerusalem. "Given the animosity between Jews and Samaritans, it is not surprising that the Samaritans refuse to show hospitality" to Jesus.[5] As the Galilean ministry started with rejection in Nazareth, so his journey to Jerusalem similarly starts with rejection.[6] This is the first mention of Samaritans in Luke and the only negative one, as the travel narrative will include two stories involving Samaritans. The first and most famous is Jesus's parable about the good Samaritan—a foil for the lawyer who wants to justify not loving his neighbor (10:25–37). The second is when Jesus heals ten lepers and only one comes back to say thank you—Luke notes it was a Samaritan, again working as a foil to the other nine (17:11–19).

But the key encounter in this scene comes in the reaction of the disciples to the rejection and Jesus's response. The disciples James and John ask, "Lord, do you want us to call fire down from heaven to destroy them?" This response seems very bizarre to a modern reader. What would lead these two disciples, who have been with Jesus all along, to assume that this is an appropriate response? Simple: this is what Elijah the prophet did in a similar situation.[7] In 2 Kings 1, Elijah is feuding with King Ahaziah and has an encounter with a captain leading fifty men. "Elijah answered the captain, 'If I am a man of God, may fire come down from heaven and consume you and your fifty men!' Then fire fell from heaven and consumed the captain and his men" (2 Kgs 1:10). If Jesus is a prophet like Elijah, whom he talked with on the Mount of Transfiguration, why wouldn't he do what Elijah did when encountering those opposing God's prophet? Because Jesus has not come to recapitulate the ministry of Elijah (or Moses for that matter) but to surpass it. Jesus is a prophet in the line of Moses, and to some extent Elijah, but he is bringing a new message, a progressive and radical message of good news that expands the kingdom of God, where the outsiders become insiders. This is a theme throughout Luke-Acts but is specifically emphasized during the travel narrative.[8] Samaritans become one of the first people groups to accept the good news after the disciples leave Jerusalem (Acts 8:1–25). As we have seen before, this is not the only time Luke will

---

5. Parsons, *Luke*, 168.

6. Tannehill, *Gospel According to Luke*, 230.

7. As evidence that this is how early readers understood this reference, Parsons notes some scribes who inserted "as Elijah did" in this passage (*Luke*, 168).

8. Tannehill notes that Elijah is both a prototype and an antitype for Jesus, with the latter being emphasized from ch. 9 on (*Gospel According to Luke*, 230).

plant a seed in his Gospel that he plans to come back to more fully in Acts. Jesus rebukes the disciples, making his diversion from the ministry of Elijah clear, and they continue on to another village.

DISCIPLESHIP AND THE COST OF FOLLOWING JESUS

Once the prophetic corrective to the violent judgment of enemies is levied, we encounter our first theme of the teaching of Jesus during the travel narrative: discipleship and the costs that come with it. It is a strategic plot device and a significant challenge to the reader, that after the climactic scene of the Galilean ministry (the transfiguration), a miraculous healing, and the prediction of both his death and his journey to Jerusalem, Luke would include a litany of would-be disciples who *do not* follow Jesus for various reasons. One might think that it is here, at the outset of the journey to Jerusalem, that the narrative emphasis would be on gaining as many disciples as possible; by contrast, Luke emphasizes the difficulty of the call.

Johnson notes how regularly Jesus is said to address disciples during the travel narrative (Luke 10:23; 11:1; 12:22; 16:1; 17:1, 22; 18:1).[9] He will at times challenge them with extremely difficult expectations, such as the need to "hate" their families and carry their cross in order to be his disciple (14:26–27). He will also send them out with power to do the sorts of things he was doing, noting that he is sending them "like lambs among wolves" (10:3). And he will also teach them how to pray (11:1–13).

Indeed, discipleship is a key focus for Luke. Jesus is both teaching his companions in the narrative and inviting readers to participate in his way of the kingdom as disciples. Following Jesus as a disciple is a tall task in the harsh world of the first-century Greco-Roman world, with all of the distractions and competing forces. Luke wants the reader to know the highly challenging and exclusive call of following Jesus—even taking up one's cross daily (9:23).

KINGDOM TEACHING

A second teaching emphasis of Jesus during the journey to Jerusalem is the kingdom of God. This is admittedly a bit of a "catch-all" category with a good degree of variety, which sometimes is hard to distinguish from

---

9. Johnson, *Gospel of Luke*, 164.

PART 2: INITIATION

Jesus's teaching on discipleship. In addition, these emphases are communicated and reinforced not only through traditional teaching sections but also through encounters Jesus has with people and parables he shares in response. There are numerous topics we might think of as subcategories as Jesus teaches about his kingdom. For example, it regularly includes teachings on reversal, or what we might describe as "the upside-down kingdom." Jesus compares the kingdom of God to a mustard seed: small but growing into a significant tree (Luke 13:18–19); and to yeast that works its way through a large batch of dough (13:21). Jesus tells a parable about a prideful Pharisee, whose prayer is rejected, compared to a humble tax collector, whose prayer is accepted (18:9–14). And Jesus welcomes and embraces babies and little children, despite the rebuke of his disciples, saying "whoever does not receive the kingdom of God like a little child will never enter it" (18:15–17).

Jesus also teaches regularly on wealth and the kingdom of God. Jesus tells parables about a rich fool who tears down barns to build bigger ones (12:13–21) and a rich man and a poor man (Lazarus) who both die. The rich man goes to Hades because "in [his] lifetime [he] received good things," while Lazarus goes to Abraham's side (16:19–31). The clear indictment of the rich without much explanation here is telling. It is in line with the other teachings of Jesus on this topic, though. In 18:18–30, Jesus encounters a rich man who inquires about eternal life. While the man insists he has kept the commandments, Jesus challenges him to sell everything, give to the poor, and come back and follow Jesus. Again we see Jesus's challenging words, his prophetic critique, against wealth, as he says, "How hard it is for the rich to enter the kingdom of God" (18:24).

This story is followed not long after by a similar story in Jericho where another rich man, named Zacchaeus, a chief tax collector, also seeks out Jesus (19:1–10). Zacchaeus, in stark contrast to the rich man in chapter 18, does not declare his righteousness but, rather, shows Jesus hospitality and vows to pay back whatever he has stolen from people. This kingdom teaching combines a prophetic critique of wealth with the upside-down nature of Jesus's kingdom in that the tax collector, despite the disapproval of "all the people," repents, acts righteously, and has Jesus say of him, "Today salvation has come to this house, because this man, too, is a son of Abraham. For the Son of Man came to seek and to save the lost" (19:9–10).[10]

---

10. This is the third of four occurrences of the critic response type scenes in Luke-Acts. See Fox, *Hermeneutics of Social Identity*, 78–88.

The Journey

JUDGMENT AND APOCALYPTIC

Another teaching emphasis that becomes especially pronounced during the journey to Jerusalem is judgment, sometimes combined with a similar feature, apocalyptic. These terms need some clarification. Judgment typically has a negative connotation in our modern world, specifically when it comes to religion, the Bible, and thinking of the judgment of God. This comes, at least in part, from the modern theological view of atonement that says people are sinners and they deserve God's wrath, but Jesus's act of death and resurrection spares us from this judgment. While there is some truth to this approach in Scripture, it is a much too truncated summary of the saving work of Jesus. It is better to see the gospel (or good news)[11] as the fullness of God's redemptive work primarily in Jesus's life and mission. Note that numerous characters talk about good news (or gospel) early in Luke: the angel to both Zechariah and the shepherds (1:19; 2:10), John's preaching (3:18), Jesus at the beginning of his ministry in Luke 4. Jesus begins preaching the gospel eighteen chapters before his arrest and crucifixion. If "the gospel" refers only to Jesus's death and resurrection, then what was Jesus proclaiming? He does not begin to predict his death until Luke 9.

As you can see, the shortened form of this presentation of the gospel casts judgment in a negative light. I suggest it is more accurate to see judgment as human accountability to God, both positive and negative.[12] From the perspective of the faithful in the Bible, God's judgment was almost always a good thing. If you are a faithful servant of God, like Zechariah and Elizabeth, Mary, Simeon, and Anna, who are living under the oppression of Roman rule, you hope God will show up and judge both you and your wicked oppressors justly. As Mary sings about in the Magnificat, the rich getting their due and the poor being lifted up are judgments the faithful of God long for. This is not pettiness or bloodthirsty revenge against one's enemies but, rather, trusting God to make the injustices of the world right. So we must divest ourselves from an overly pejorative view of God's judgment. At the same time, the judgment sections of Jesus's teaching, while perhaps uncomfortable to us, call us to examine ourselves and our response to him and his call on our lives, as they did the original readers. That is part of Jesus's role as the prophet. God holding people accountable for how they live

---

11. The Gospel of Luke will not use the noun εὐαγγέλιον but will use the verb form, εὐαγγελίζω, ten times.
12. Milne, "Judgment."

and how they treat people is one of the most robust themes in Scripture. God is a God of lavishing love, and he leads with mercy and grace. Yet he does call us and challenge us to live faithful lives. Part of God being a loving parent is calling his children to faithfulness and then helping them do it.

I know there has been a lot of really bad judgmentalism in the history of the Christian church. In light of this, it can make reading texts that emphasize the judgment of God difficult. Two things we need to keep in mind. First, Jesus is speaking primarily to religious people who have a sense for the accountability of God in the world. This is not new to them. The leaders readily co-opt this language against others, so Jesus is oftentimes using the judgmental language to challenge those in power. Second, remember the wonderful thread of grace that runs through Jesus's teachings. Jesus is calling people back to the love, grace, and forgiveness of God. Many of his parables end with banquets or parties. In Luke, God is the God of lavish parties when people repent. This must color the way we read these judgment sections. Despite a difficult history in the church, I hope Jesus can help us heal from that wounding and see the good and just nature of God's faithful administration of accountability.

Second, we must gain a better understanding of apocalyptic. While few topics are as confounding to modern readers of the New Testament as apocalyptic literature and apocalypse as a theological category, these were common in the ancient world.[13] In addition, many scholars of first-century Judaism have written extensively on this topic in ways that can be very helpful.[14] An apocalyptic theological outlook can best be summarized as teachings or literature that usually involve angels disclosing a transcendent reality and concern future judgment.[15] This content is often highly symbolic and strange, lending itself to a dramatic communication style. While the tendency of certain modern readers tends to be to view apocalyptic sections of Scripture—such as the book of Revelation but also the apocalyptic teachings of Jesus—as futuristic foretelling regarding world leaders and global politics, we must remember that the primary audience is the original recipients of these writings in *their* time, and thus these sections are

---

13. Pitre helpfully argues that we do well to see this word as referring to a genre, a theological worldview, and a kind of eschatology ("Apocalypticism," 24).

14. Consider, for example, Gorman, *Reading Revelation Responsibly*; Osborne, *Revelation*; Peterson, *Reversed Thunder*.

15. This is my summary of a much larger and more complex definition in Collins, *Apocalyptic Imagination*, 4–5, 9. For more on apocalyptic, see Hanson, *Dawn of Apocalyptic*; Rowland, *Open Heaven*; Horsley, *Revolt of the Scribes*.

primarily intended to communicate to them. Reading Scripture as specifically addressed to the modern individual reader is called solipsism and is a grievous hermeneutical error; it must be avoided in favor of better, more faithful readings of God's word.

Jesus has a number of teachings in the journey to Jerusalem that emphasize judgment, and at times these incorporate apocalyptic theology as well. He also regularly pairs positive judgment to the faithful with negative judgment to the unfaithful. Shortly after the travel narrative begins, Jesus pronounces woes on several towns, Chorazin and Bethsaida, who fail to repent despite the outpouring of miracles done among them. Jesus predicts their spiritual downfall (10:15). This is contrasted with those who accept the disciples Jesus sends out, who have the kingdom of God in their midst (10:9). In 12:1–12, Jesus warns his disciples about the hypocrisy of the Pharisees, challenging them to fear God, not humanity.[16] As God has control over eternal spiritual destinies and is worthy of fear, he is also readily able to remember and protect his people from danger and persecution—even life-threatening persecution, something the disciples will experience firsthand in Acts—when it comes.

Similarly, Jesus will teach about being watchful (12:35–48). When a master returns to his servants, he will reward the faithful who are ready and watching but will punish the ones who are wasteful and ill-prepared. He also urges his followers to enter through the narrow door (13:22–30) and says that many will try to but, despite claiming friendship with "the owner of the house," will not be let in.

Jesus's teaching on judgment in 17:20–37 is rich with apocalyptic imagery. The Pharisees ask when the kingdom of God will come. Jesus corrects them, as they do not understand the nature of his kingdom. Nor, apparently, do his disciples. Jesus will speak of the day of the Son of Man and will cite the Old Testament stories of Noah and Lot, both times of the faithful few being spared while the many unfaithful also experienced divine accountability. Jesus mentions some being taken and others left, as well as vultures (or eagles) gathering around a dead body. These passages are cryptic and

---

16. "Fear" is another word that is often rife with negative connotations in our world. While fear is viewed as a spiritual deficit in our world—indeed the Bible regularly encourages people not to fear—the fear of God is often misunderstood. The emphasis here should be understood as reverence for the awesomeness of God. Here, as in other places, a verse that starts out seeming to emphasize negative judgment (i.e., "fear him ... who has the authority to throw you into hell") transitions to the great worth of people compared to sparrows and God's ability and willingness to save them.

confusing; commentators disagree on specifically how these images should be understood. The larger point, though, is clear: God will hold people accountable for how they live, and he is able to rescue his people from the clutches of evil and danger. However evil the world might be, God has not given up on the world, and the coming of Jesus is as a clarion call to repent and live in harmony with God's ways.

There is a healthy place for these prophetic teachings of Jesus on judgment in our lives. May we read the judgment texts in Luke as good news: as a call to open our eyes and wake up to areas in our lives that might have fallen asleep; as a reminder that God's hand is not short in rescuing his people from the danger of the world; and as an assurance that ultimately it is God who is responsible for righting the wrongs of the world and bringing forth justice.

CONFLICT WITH THE POWERS

A final emphasis of Jesus's teaching during the travel narrative is conflict with the powers and authorities. This is an escalating motif that builds over the course of the narrative in order to prepare the reader for Jesus's ultimate ordeal in Jerusalem. Luke is very intentional in including increased references to persecution and conflict.

The conflict motif comes in various forms. In Luke 11:14–22, some accuse Jesus of casting out demons by Beelzebul, to which Jesus responds by defending himself.[17] Similarly, the Pharisees challenge Jesus about not following handwashing rituals (11:37–54). Jesus responds with a prophetic critique about the condition of the inside being more important than that of the outside, before pronouncing woes on the Pharisees. While they meticulously give, they do not practice justice, mercy, and love. Jesus challenges them on a number of other elements before the climax of his prophetic critique, when he says, "Woe to you, because you build tombs for the prophets, and it was your ancestors who killed them" (11:47). While the Pharisees and teachers of the law honor the prophets by building tombs, thus honoring their memory, they have more in common with those who persecuted and killed the prophets. As both a sign of the conflict between Jesus and the leaders as well as a critical piece of foreshadowing, Luke reports that these

---

17. Beelzebul is a reference to a Philistine deity, which is seen in the NT as a reference to the demonic (BDAG 173).

two groups began to oppose him fiercely (11:53–54). Indeed, the tension is building even early in the journey to Jerusalem.

Jesus also anticipates the kind of treatment his followers will encounter. He tells of them being dragged before the synagogues, rulers, and authorities, as will occur in Acts 3–5, and that the Holy Spirit will give them words to say (Luke 12:11–12). Likewise, followers of Jesus should expect division because of the radical call he has placed on their lives (12:49–53). And in at least one occasion, we see Jesus's specific conflict with Herod. The Pharisees warn him that Herod wants to kill him; Jesus responds, saying, "Go tell that fox, 'I will keep on driving out demons and healing people today and tomorrow, and on the third day I will reach my goal.' In any case, I must press on today and tomorrow and the next day—for surely no prophet can die outside Jerusalem!" (13:32–33). We see here the testament of the importance of Jerusalem and its location for the climactic event of Jesus the prophet. But we also see Jesus's recalcitrant response to Herod. He follows this statement up by both a prophetic critique of Jerusalem—those who kill the prophets—and how he desires to gather them under his wing, a symbol of protection (13:34–35). This scene once again looks ahead to Jesus's entrance into Jerusalem at the end of the journey but also his conflict with the powers.

AT THE PHARISEE'S TABLE

As we close the discussion of the journey to Jerusalem and the teaching emphases of Jesus, let's look at one story that nicely combines all four of these emphases into one string of encounters.

In Luke 14, what might be considered the center of the journey to Jerusalem section, Jesus goes to a Pharisee's house for dinner. Despite this hospitality, something we have come to expect in Jesus's ministry,[18] the narrator tells us that since it is the Sabbath, Jesus is being carefully watched. Jesus experiences *conflict* with the Pharisees and the teachers of the law as he heals a man with abnormal swelling, before rebuking his critics. He then offers a *kingdom teaching* in the form of a parable about a wedding feast and challenges them to take the lower seats as opposed to the more important seats, emphasizing humility, as well as challenging them to invite to their parties the poor, the crippled, the blind, and the lame, a classic Lukan motif. If you do this, he says, you will be rewarded by God as he *judges* at the

18. Luke 5:27–32; 7:36–50; 9:10–17; 10:38–42; 11:37–52.

resurrection. He follows this with the story of a banquet, where many are invited, but like the ones who were called to be *disciples* back in chapter 10, many make excuses and do not come. Yet, the master desires that his house be full, so he sends them to the streets to compel whomsoever will come.

This scene is important as it works as something of a midpoint on the travel narrative for Luke. We might view it as a sort of "day in the life" for Jesus, as so many of the themes are wrapped together in this series of teachings by Jesus. Again, the reader is challenged to listen to Jesus, to live a radically different life, to be Jesus's disciple, and to trust Jesus as the prophet from God.

As Jesus approaches Jerusalem, the journey nears its end. Soon the prophet will enter the city, setting the stage for the final ordeal. What the reader has been waiting for is about to come to pass.

But a few things have to happen before we arrive at the climax. This is our hero's approach on the way to his final battle.

DISCUSSION QUESTIONS

1. Which of the four teaching themes of Jesus in this section—discipleship, the kingdom of God, judgment and apocalyptic, or conflict with the powers—resonates most with you?

2. Why do you think the journey to Jerusalem is an important part of Jesus's Hero's Journey?

3. Can you think of a significant journey you have had to take in your life that might work proverbially like a journey to Jerusalem?

8

The Approach: Jesus's Final Week

Heroes, having made the adjustment to the Special World, now go on to seek its heart. They pass into an intermediate region between the border and the very center of the Hero's Journey. . . . This is the Approach to the Inmost Cave, where soon they will encounter supreme wonder and terror. It is time to make final preparations for the central ordeal of the adventure."

—Christopher Vogler, *Writer's Journey*, 169

From then on he taught each day in the Temple. The high priests, religion scholars, and the leaders of the people were trying their best to find a way to get rid of him. But with the people hanging on every word he spoke, they couldn't come up with anything.

—Luke 19:47-48 MSG

MANY HERO STORIES HAVE a buildup to the final battle. Some authors refer to this as "the Approach to the Inmost Cave."[1] Like a mountain climber who

---

1. Vogler, *Writer's Journey*, 169.

has established a base camp in the mountains, he is "about to make the final assault on the highest peak."[2]

The author of Luke's Gospel, too, has an interest in dwelling on the final preparations before the climax. In his final week—Sunday to Sunday—Jesus will spend several of those days teaching and performing prophetic acts in Jerusalem before his arrest. This last week of Jesus's life has been memorialized by Christians celebrating the week that leads up to Easter. Jesus makes his approach to the final ordeal.

The entry into Jerusalem is something of a climactic scene in Luke. It has been in view since the journey to Jerusalem was officially announced in 9:51, and the reader has been reminded many times.[3] What is more, this scene is climactic because of the buildup right before. In the journey to Jerusalem, two of the last three scenes have to do with the kingship of Jesus. In the first (18:35–43), a blind beggar is sitting beside the road and hears Jesus and those with him approaching. Having asked and learned that Jesus was approaching, the man shouts, "Jesus, Son of David, have mercy on me" (18:38). The healing of this blind man fits perfectly with the mission of Jesus, who associates his ministry with giving sight to the blind in 4:18 and 7:22. Jesus welcomes and embraces people of all kinds who respond in faith, particularly those whom people have traditionally rejected (18:39).[4]

However, there is also a larger thematic impact on the narrative. The identification of Jesus as the Son of David is not new. The angel made clear to Mary in 1:32–33 that "God will give him the throne of his father David, and he will reign over Jacob's descendants forever; his kingdom will never end."[5] But Luke intentionally reminds the reader here of Jesus's kingly identity in the form of a brash and courageous blind man who is not too proud to yell out for the Son of David to notice him. Although some want to silence the beggar and these kingly claims, Jesus has the man brought to him and heals him, showing not only that God's kingdom has room for the blind but that Jesus accepts the title "Son of David."

Additionally, the last scene before Jesus enters Jerusalem records him telling a parable. Variously labeled as the parable of the ten minas or, more

---

2. Vogler, *Writer's Journey*, 169.

3. Luke 9:53; 13:22; 17:11; 18:31; 19:11.

4. In this way, the story is similar to the story of the little children with Jesus in 18:15–17.

5. Also Joseph is regularly identified as in the line of David (1:27; 2:4). David shows up in Jesus's genealogy (3:31) and in the canticles (1:69), and he is a somewhat regular referent in Jesus's ministry (6:3; 20:41–44).

The Approach: Jesus's Final Week

traditionally, the parable of the pounds (19:11–27), it seems to have a clear connection with Jesus entering Jerusalem, not only because it directly precedes it but because the introduction states, "While they were listening to this, he went on to tell them a parable, because he was near Jerusalem and the people thought that the kingdom of God was going to appear at once" (19:11). This parable is one of the most complex that Jesus tells, leading to numerous, even contradictory interpretations of it. Is the man appointed king who trusts people with resources and holds them accountable, rewarding the faithful and judging the unfaithful, Jesus?[6] Or is the new king a foil, highlighting his wicked and harsh judgment to be radically contrasted with the mercy of Jesus?[7] Or is it making a historical point about Herod Archelaus and his tumultuous reign in this area?[8] Additionally, is this parable about the time between Jesus's ascension and return or a more immediate commentary on the narrative?[9] As you can see, this parable is rife with complexity.

Here it is important to remember, as a point of hermeneutical and interpretive practice, that parables are not allegories with a strict one-to-one correspondence.[10] In Luke 18:1–8, where Jesus tells the parable of the persistent widow who seeks justice from an unjust judge, we are not to ascribe the hideous and evil attributes of the judge figure to God. Rather, as the woman approached the judge, we are to pray earnestly and boldly. The logic of the parable is if this judge is moved by the persistence of this widow, how much more is a loving God moved by our prayers?[11] Likewise here, the slave's picture of the king as a hard man, reaping what he did not sow, need not be applied as accurate portrayals of Jesus or God. Instead, the important theme consistent with Luke's narrative is Jesus, the king, is rejected by some and not others.

Given the narrative of Luke up to this point and the content that follows, I hold that the parable of the pounds is primarily a parable emphasizing God holding people accountable for their actions—specifically here

---

6. Johnson, *Gospel of Luke*, 294.

7. Parsons, *Luke*, 280–82.

8. Bock, *Luke*, 2:1525–26; *Ant.* 17.8.1 §188; 17.9.3 §222; 17.11.4 §317; Josephus, *J.W.* 2.6.1 §80; 2.6.3 §93.

9. For the first view, see Bock, *Luke*, 2:1525. For the second view, see Johnson, *Gospel of Luke*, 293–94; Green, *Gospel of Luke*, 674–75.

10. Snodgrass, *Stories with Intent*, 8–9.

11. This method, called *qal vahomer* (from the lesser to the greater), is a feature of Jewish hermeneutics of the time.

Part 2: Initiation

either recognizing or rejecting the prophet-king, Jesus—and a commentary on what is about to happen in Jerusalem, namely, the rejection of Jesus by some. The theme of God holding people accountable is not new; as we have seen, this has been a primary teaching emphasis of Jesus in the journey to Jerusalem and will continue to be emphasized the last week of Jesus's life. Luke wants his reader to know that we are responsible for how we respond to the Son of God who has come. Whether we accept or reject, both have consequences. Acceptance means discipleship and significant cost, which has been laid out, but also salvation and participation in God's kingdom. Rejection means separation and being cut off. Nearly every group we encounter in Luke has people from each category. Those held primarily accountable in Luke for rejecting Jesus, who conspire to arrest, and then mock, torture, and kill him, are not the crowds but those of the relatively small group of elite Jewish leaders in Jerusalem (absent the Pharisees) with whom the conflict with Jesus continues to escalate. The crowds or the Jews at large are not primarily responsible, as they flock to listen to him teach and hang on his every word (19:48).[12]

ENTERING JERUSALEM

For Jesus's entry into Jerusalem, Luke uses the rhetorical strategy of *ekphrasis*, that is, using vivid and descriptive speech to paint a visual picture for the reader.[13] Having this visual in mind, as well as the importance of the religious and cultural symbols, is important to grasp the full impact of this scene. To do that, we need to discuss some political history.

Pontius Pilate was the governor of Judea from 26 to 36 CE. Pilate lived in Herod's palace in Caesarea Maritima on the coast, but for the Passover, Pilate traveled to and stayed in Jerusalem. Passover was one of the pilgrimage festivals, where Jewish people would travel to Jerusalem for the celebration, resulting in the population of the city increasing to over a million. And if there was ever a time that zealous Jewish people might band

---

12. Some have accused Luke of anti-Semitism. See Sanders, "Parable of the Pounds." I do not see that present in Luke, who is fairly specific on placing blame for the crucifixion of Jesus (i.e., on the leaders), and even when a broader responsibility is cast (e.g., Acts 3:13–15), repentance and grace are offered, as opposed to a harsh response. For further discussion, see Tannehill, *Gospel According to Luke*, 81–85, 161; Green, *Gospel of Luke*, 676.

13. Hermogenes, "On Ecphrasis," 86. Parsons highlights a number of these instances of ekphrasis in Luke-Acts (*Luke*, 155, 321).

The Approach: Jesus's Final Week

together to overthrow their Roman captors, wouldn't it be during the feast that celebrated God miraculously intervening and leading his people out of slavery from a harsh, foreign, ruling power? So, Pilate needed to be in Jerusalem, along with a significant Roman military presence. At some point before the Passover, Pilate traveled from Caesarea in the west, on the coast of the Mediterranean, traveling east and entering Jerusalem from the west side of town. And how does the Roman governor of Judea, a representative of Caesar, enter Jerusalem? With all the pomp and circumstance of royalty, of course.[14] Riding a warhorse, adorned in shiny armor and the trappings of Roman rule, with as many as a thousand soldiers with him, Pilate would have entered Jerusalem in style. The important people in the city, the social, political, and religious elite would dress in their appropriate attire and greet the leader as he approached.[15]

Luke's audience would have been aware of the well-known tradition of celebratory welcomes of Roman governors, kings, and dignitaries into a city.[16] And while we cannot know for sure, we can imagine a dramatic scenario that at the same time, on the same day (Sunday), at the beginning of Passover week, as Pilate rides into town with all of his pomp and circumstance, greeted by the elite of the city in ostentatious display, on the other side of the city, approaching from the east, at the Mount of Olives, another king is approaching the city, with trappings and symbols of a much different sort.

As this other king, Jesus, nears Jerusalem, he sends two disciples ahead of him to retrieve not a warhorse but a young donkey. Why a donkey? Several times in the Hebrew Scriptures, kings are said to be riding donkeys (or mules [1 Kgs 1:32–33; Zech 9:9]). The donkey has never been ridden, a possible hint at kingship as well.[17] Despite the kingly connections, the visual of Jesus riding a young donkey contrasts starkly with how we imagine Pilate—comically so. The people spread their cloaks on the road, another image of kingship from the Hebrew Scriptures (2 Kgs 9:13).[18] Jesus rides the young animal into Jerusalem, where "the whole crowd of disciples began

---

14. This is best argued by Kinman: "Jesus' 'Triumphal Entry'"; Kinman, "Parousia."
15. Kinman, "Parousia," 281–82.
16. Kinman, "Parousia," 289.
17. Bock, *Luke*, 2:1554; Kinman, "Parousia," 287. For an argument against this view, see Fitzmyer, *Luke X–XXIV*, 1249.
18. Parsons suggests that the tone here is of a nationalistic king, which contributes to his view that this is a "fundamental misunderstanding" by the crowd (*Luke*, 281–83).

joyfully to praise God in loud voices for all the miracles they had seen" (Luke 19:37). Remember that the working of signs and wonders is a key element of the role of the prophet, again emphasized here (as in 4:18–19; 7:22–23). The people quote Ps 118; however, Luke has inserted the word "king" (Gk: βασιλεὺς): "Blessed is *the king* who comes in the name of the Lord!" (19:38). And who are these people? They are the crowds who have been listening to and following Jesus. Largely poor and disenfranchised, but also undoubtably some others as well, this crowd is substantially different from the city's elite greeting Pilate. Predictably, as we have been primed to expect from the two previous stories of kingship (blind beggar and the parable of the pounds), some people, in this case the Pharisees, object to what the people are saying. They see the imagery and recognize the bold messianic statement being made. "Teacher, rebuke your disciples!" "I tell you," he replied, "if they keep quiet, the stones will cry out" (19:39–40). Parsons says, "Like John the Baptist before him (3:8), Jesus declares that if humans fail to bear witness to this kind of king, the very stones themselves will cry out."[19]

In stark contrast to Pilate, Jesus arrives as a king not ready to flex military muscle but as a humble king, welcomed by the poor, not on a warhorse but on a young donkey. What is sometimes called the triumphal entry is anything but; rather, it is a prophetic critique of the military might of Rome and a strong message that Jesus is a different kind of king, "lowly and riding on a donkey."[20]

As this scene concludes, Jesus weeps over the city, predicting its destruction.[21] This is reminiscent of 13:34–35. As has been obvious in the narrative up to this point, some accept Jesus, while others reject him. His ultimate rejection is soon coming, in this very city, the culmination of the trajectory of the story. Luke gives an uninterrupted flow as the prophet enters the city, weeps over it, cleanses the temple, and then takes occupation

19. Parsons, *Luke*, 285.

20. Parsons argues that the crowd has fundamentally misunderstood Jesus and his kingship, expecting a triumphant king. Rather than a prophetic critique on Rome, he sees instead the critique of the crowd who misunderstands Jesus's type of kingship (*Luke*, 282–85).

21. Kinman suggests that this pronouncement is a direct result of Jerusalem failing to give Jesus a proper kingly welcome ("Parousia"). It seems more likely to me, though, that Jesus's pronouncement is a further critique of the dichotomy between the peace that he embodies and the violence of the way of the world, which will ultimately result in the destruction of Jerusalem by the Romans. This is how I view Luke 13:34–35 and 23:28–31 as well.

The Approach: Jesus's Final Week

of it by teaching there every day. Let's look at these scenes and the emphases in the ministry of Jesus during his last week.

TEACHING AND MINISTRY EMPHASES: THE FINAL WEEK

As the other Gospels do, Luke records Jesus cleansing the temple once he comes to Jerusalem. However, while he expanded and emphasized the kingly nature of Jesus in the triumphal entry, he downplays the cleansing of the temple, delimiting it to only two verses. In Jesus's prophetic critique of the buying and selling, "'My house shall be a house of prayer'; but you have made it a den of robbers" (Luke 19:46), he eliminates the phrase "for all nations" that Mark includes. The temple will not have a significant religious future for gentiles; instead, the temple will be a meeting location for spreading the gospel. Jesus embodies that here, making it the central location of his teaching the last week, as "every day he was teaching at the temple" (19:47). It is also a place of danger, as the chief priests and teachers of the law (but conspicuously not the Pharisees) try to kill him.

Our first glimpse into the teaching Jesus does at the temple the last week of his life continues an emphasis we saw building in the journey to Jerusalem, conflict. This will be by far the most common emphasis this last week.[22] Luke wants the reader to realize the prophetic challenge that Jesus embodies in his teaching and actions but also the increasingly violent response of the leaders. More specific than just conflict, though, we might more accurately describe this issue as "the acceptance and rejection of God's Prophet."[23]

The first four scenes are all specifically focused on this. In 20:2, the chief priests, teachers of the law, and elders ask him, "Tell us by what authority you are doing these things. . . . Who gave you this authority?" The question is likely concerned with both Jesus's cleansing of the temple and his occupation and teaching in the temple; the leaders were the ones who could grant permission to teach in the temple.[24] Jesus cleverly centers his

---

22. Of the eleven scenes from 20:1–22:46, more than half are specifically centered on this issue of Jesus's conflict with different powers in Jerusalem.

23. Johnson, *Gospel of Luke*, 307.

24. Johnson, *Gospel of Luke*, 308. Johnson also mentions this could be part of the clever setup of the authorities, for if Jesus claims a divine authority it could be a change of blasphemy.

PART 2: INITIATION

response around John's baptism, the time understood as the beginning of God's activity in Luke-Acts.[25] This scene emphasizes both the importance of John in God's plan of redemption and salvation, and the authorities' failure to recognize God's activity in their midst, both with John and with Jesus.[26]

Jesus follows this with the parable of the vineyard directed toward the people, which the authorities apparently overhear. They then seek to arrest him (20:9–19). Jesus is not a passive sage dispensing wisdom, rather, he is an aggressive prophetic teacher presenting a challenging critique to the authorities. "Above all, of course, the plot to kill the heir and the carrying out of that murder point directly to the rejection of Jesus and his execution."[27] And as Luke is fond of doing, the parable serves as a sort of narrative commentary on the events unfolding in the Gospel up to this point and soon to come.

The next series of scenes all involve Jesus experiencing controversy with different "philosophical schools" of Judaism.[28] The first two scenes in this series involve paying taxes to Rome and questions about the resurrection and marriage with the Sadducees. Both are "bad-faith" questions, setups in order to trap Jesus by what he says.[29] Several times we have seen—and will continue to see—Jesus experiencing conflict with the authorities and the crowd being a barrier from them arresting him on the spot. Here, though, Jesus' wisdom and ingenuity as a teacher allow him to best the traps of his accusers. Jesus also warns against the teachers of the law (20:45–47) and challenges the wealth of the rich, by contrast elevating the tiny offering of a poor widow (21:1–4). These scenes of conflict taken as a whole make a resounding statement that Jesus, the prophet and true Son of God, is at odds with the leadership of the Jews—not with the crowds or the Jewish people as a whole and not even at this point in the narrative with the Pharisees—and like the prophets before him, is to be killed in Jerusalem.

And it is in this section of the narrative where the dramatic plot that leads to Jesus's arrest and execution increases tremendously. But first, Luke presents Jesus's teaching in his second lengthy apocalyptic teaching in the

---

25. See also Acts 1:21–22.
26. Johnson, *Gospel of Luke*, 308.
27. Johnson, *Gospel of Luke*, 309.
28. Johnson, *Gospel of Luke*, 316–17.
29. While the question of paying taxes seems to have no right answer, the Sadducees do not believe in a resurrection (20:27), so their entire scenario is created as an elaborate sham.

book so far. The first was back in 17:30–37 regarding the coming kingdom. This section starts with critique of the temple. Once again, this section is long, somewhat cryptic, and hard to understand for modern readers and, thus, likely to be misunderstood and misapplied.[30] While many good commentaries engage in detail with the images and intertextual echoes,[31] our narrative-driven task here will be to focus on the overarching point for Luke, namely, Jesus predicting the destruction of Jerusalem and the ultimate presence of God even in terrible times. We also must remember where this story is going; rather than "doom and gloom" with death and corrupt power winning the day, Acts tells of a Holy Spirit who leads radical missionary initiatives to take God's redemptive gospel to the ends of earth, converting all kinds of people, including Jewish leaders, outsiders, and even Roman soldiers.

THE MECHANISMS OF BETRAYAL

Luke presents the dramatic unfolding of how Jesus comes to be arrested throughout the narrative. The ingredients of this are as follows. First, Jesus has predicted his death several times (Luke 12:49–50; 13:33–34; 16:31; 17:25; 18:31–33; 19:14), so despite the disciples' ongoing surprise when it occurs, the reader is not surprised. Second, conflict has been a major emphasis in the life and ministry of Jesus that has continued to increase up until the last week of his life, coming to the point of intended violence (19:47). Third, there are two barriers in the way of the authorities arresting him and dispensing their violence: Jesus's own cleverness in avoiding their traps but, more importantly, the large crowds around Jesus in the city who hang on his words and would intervene if the authorities tried to arrest him there. However, fourth, Luke has told us that although Jesus spends his days in the city teaching the people, at night he retreats with his disciples to the Mount of Olives to stay (21:37–38). This would be a normal practice. Since the city is so crowded because of travelers for the Passover, it is easier to camp outside the city. So why don't the authorities just arrest him there? Because there are so many people camping outside the city, it would be

---

30. Johnson's warning is important to keep in mind here, avoiding both the millenarian speculation about modern prophetic fulfillment as well as the historian speculation about what Jesus might have actually said, as both distract us from Luke's larger narrative purposes (*Gospel of Luke*, 324–25).

31. See Johnson, *Gospel of Luke*, 324–31; Parsons, *Luke*, 299–306.

Part 2: Initiation

impossible to find Jesus among all of those people in the dark. So finally, the solution is Judas, who, being one of the Twelve, knows where Jesus and the other disciples camp. He offers to lead the authorities there so they can arrest Jesus in quiet, without the multitude of loyal people intervening.

Luke is careful to dispense this information slowly over the course of the approach. The reader learns the details of Judas' betrayal in 22:3–6, which they had been warned about back in 6:16. The event comes to a dramatic climax at the Last Supper, the last chance Jesus has to communicate kingdom teaching to his disciples before he is arrested. It is there that he confronts Judas and predicts his betrayal. We also have a prediction of Peter's denial, more drama for the ordeal.

And so we see, as Jesus is praying on the Mount of Olives (Luke does not specify Gethsemane), a crowd approaches, led by Judas (22:39–48). The disciples resist, one cutting off the ear of the servant of the high priest (22:49–50). We know, then, that it was the priestly leadership behind this arrest. In the midst of being arrested, Jesus heals the ear of his enemy, once again demonstrating the upside-down kingdom he represents, radically different than the economy of violence and revenge represented by the world and its powers (22:51).

And now we are here, at the climax, the apotheosis, the ordeal. We have come with our hero nearly twenty-two chapters on this Hero's Journey, and we are now ready for the final battle. But this battle is different, as this Hero's Journey is different.

DISCUSSION QUESTIONS

1. Which of the scenes in Jesus's final week is your favorite and why?

2. How does the juxtaposition of Jesus's and Pilate's entrances into Jerusalem sit with you? Are there other things you think the author wants us to take from that scene?

3. As you think about the mechanisms of betrayal present in the Gospel of Luke, how does it make you feel?

4. Is there a time in your life where you have been on the approach of a climactic event that allows you to relate to the hero at the end of a journey?

9

The Ordeal

The Christian cross is the most telling symbol of the mythological passage into the abyss of death.

—Joseph Campbell, *The Hero with a Thousand Faces*, 213

By now it was noon. The whole earth became dark, the darkness lasting three hours—a total blackout. The Temple curtain split right down the middle. Jesus called loudly, "Father, I place my life in your hands!" Then he breathed his last.

—Luke 23:46–48 MSG

EVERY STORY OF A hero journeying on a quest has an apotheosis, a climax. Campbell is fond of calling this simply *the Ordeal*. It is the final battle our hero must fight. Booker says, "It is this final struggle which is necessary for the hero to lay hold of his prize and to secure it."[1] This phase of the Hero's Journey shows its face in myriad stories throughout ancient and modern history. Indeed, it may be the most recognizable trope in the Hero's Journey

---

1. Booker, *Seven Basic Plots*, 79.

Part 2: Initiation

framework.[2] Neo does battle with Agent Smith. Luke Skywalker flies his X-wing to take down the dreaded Death Star. The heroic knight must face the ferocious dragon.

Furthermore, a common feature of the ordeal is the death and rebirth of the hero. Hollywood screenwriting consultant Christopher Vogler says, "Heroes need to die so they can be reborn. The dramatic movement that audiences enjoy more than any other is death and rebirth. In some way in every story, heroes face death or something like it: their greatest fears, the failure of an enterprise, the end of a relationship, the death of an old personality."[3] Many times in movies, this is more of a near-death experience, such as when Darth Vader obtains radar lock on Luke Skywalker's X-wing. Other times, it is real death, such as when Neo is shot and killed by Agent Smith in the hallway outside of Room 303 or when "Spielberg's E.T. dies before our eyes."[4]

These latter examples where the hero faces real death resemble the story of Jesus and the dramatic turns Luke's narrative takes to bring this to fruition. Luke reserves significant space in his narrative to tell this part of the story. The cross is an early stumbling block for people (1 Cor 1:23): how can the Messiah, a triumphant king, be sentenced to the worst, most humiliating death available? Controversy needs context. For this reason, the Gospel writers take ample space to flesh out the story of Jesus's arrest, trial, and crucifixion. Luke will do a similar thing in the book of Acts with the conversion of Paul, a foremost enemy of the Christians, who becomes its most well-known disciple, telling that story three times in Acts.[5] That Jesus is crucified at the climax of this hero story, and that this event reveals God in all of his love and beauty, is a profound mystery. As Fleming Rutledge says,

> The unique feature of the Christian proclamation is the shocking claim that God is fully acting, not only in Jesus' resurrected life, but *especially in Jesus' death on the cross*. To say the same thing in another way, the death of Jesus in and of itself would not be

---

2. Vogler writing for modern screenwriters, differentiates between the climax, or apotheosis, and the final battle or ordeal (*Writer's Journey*, 184–85). However, Campbell oftentimes thinks of them as the same.

3. Vogler, *Writer's Journey*, 183.

4. Vogler, *Writer's Journey*, 184.

5. Acts 9:1–19a; 22:1–21; 26:9–23.

anything remarkable. What is remarkable is that *the Creator of the universe is shown forth in this gruesome death.*[6]

Another key for the ordeal in Luke is that Jesus's execution is unwarranted. More than any of the other Gospels, Luke wants his readers to know that Jesus was innocent of the charges brought against him and yet died a criminal's death. Even though the reader has been along for the ministry and revelation of Jesus, the prophet, Luke continues to make it plain here.

Last, we have observed a theme in Luke that in any group of people who have an encounter with Jesus, some of them respond positively and some of them go away uninterested. This has been true for people in the synagogues (4:14–44) and rich people (18:18–30; 19:1–10), but it will become more obvious and more pronounced during Jesus's trial and death. Thus, without further ado, let us examine the ordeal in Jerusalem, the death of our hero.

PETER'S DENIAL

We ended the previous chapter by looking at the mechanism of betrayal for our hero. Judas agrees to betray Jesus by leading the soldiers of the high priest to the Mount of Olives where they can arrest Jesus without the threat of the crowd intervening. This scene is followed by one in which Peter, the most prominent of the disciples, denies Jesus (Luke 22:54–62). Peter had said dramatically the night before at the Last Supper that he was ready to go "to prison and to death" with Jesus (22:33). Despite his best intentions, here we see him deny his Lord.

While we may be tempted to be hard on Peter for his denial here, we note the conspicuous absence of the other apostles; Peter seems to be the only one willing to risk following Jesus to the place of his examination. Over the course of a couple hours, three different people accuse Peter of being with Jesus (22:56, 58, 59). Each time, Peter denies even knowing Jesus, confirming what Jesus had predicted at the Last Supper (22:33). As the last of the denials is completed the narrator says that Jesus turns and looks at Peter; certainly a moment of high drama. The scene presumes that Peter is waiting in the courtyard outside of Caiaphas' house, and as they bring Jesus outside after questioning him, Peter's third denial is finishing, the rooster crows, and Jesus looks directly at him, knowing what happened.

---

6. Rutledge, *Crucifixion*, 11–12; emphasis in original.

PART 2: INITIATION

The crowing rooster and this nonverbal connection with Jesus spark the memory for Peter; he goes out and weeps "bitterly" (22:62). This scene, with Peter's memory jogged at a specific dramatic moment, is the first of several times where memory will be an important signifier for Luke.

MOCKERY AND TRIAL

The scene then shifts to Jesus in custody of the men guarding him. They blindfold him and beat him, mocking him by saying, "Prophesy! Who hit you?" The text also says they said many other things insulting him (Luke 22:65). The mockery of Jesus in this way here is ironic, since Jesus's prophetic predictions are coming true: "He has been betrayed (22:21; cf. 22:47–53), denied 22:34; cf. 22:54–62), reckoned with transgressors (22:37; cf. 22:52), beaten and mocked (18:32; cf. 22:63)—and there is more to come."[7] While there were threats of violence before,[8] here we see, for the first time, violence poured out on the hero.

When the scene transitions again it is morning—the previous events apparently lasting all night. Luke narrates Jesus on trial before "the chief priests and the teachers of the law" (22:66). The various trials of Jesus can be a bit confusing to the casual reader, not only because of the multiple Gospel accounts but because of the numerous courts represented in the trial of Jesus. This first level is the Jewish leadership responsible for arresting Jesus, namely, the Sanhedrin (22:66). These people have been the primary ones Jesus has had conflict with since he came to Jerusalem[9] and whom he predicted in 9:22 would be responsible for killing him.[10] They question Jesus about being the Messiah, a question about which Jesus seems to be evasive (22:67–68). However, the reader knows that Luke's narrative clearly has presented Jesus as the prophet, the Messiah,[11] and Son of God.[12] So why is Jesus elusive here? The answer must be in Jesus's statements in 22:67–68—"If I tell you, you will not believe me, and if I asked you, you would not answer"—and in his recent history with the chief priests and teachers of the law; their questions are traps. They are not questioning him

---

7. Parsons, *Luke*, 325.
8. Luke 4:28–30; 13:31.
9. Luke 19:47; 20:1, 19; 22:2–4, 50–54.
10. Along with "the elders."
11. Luke 2:11, 26; 4:41; 18:36–43.
12. Luke 3:22; 9:35.

The Ordeal

in good faith—indeed their guards have beaten and mocked Jesus in the night. Rather, they seek to humiliate and kill Jesus however they can. Jesus is not interested in helping them achieve their corrupt mission. However, he does not shy away from claiming his special place as the Son of God and predicting the resurrection (22:69).[13] Jesus's words are enough to convince the council that he is guilty, and they immediately send him to Pilate (23:1).

Pontius Pilate is a historical figure we know a little something about from Roman history.[14] He was appointed governor (*prefectus*) of Judea in 26 CE by Tiberius and reigned for a decade.[15] His reputation is mixed, containing both accusations of brutality and more compassionate examples of diplomacy and compromise.[16] In Luke's Gospel, Pilate comes across as a fairly efficient governor, attempting to avoid punishing Jesus unjustly but also seeking to appease the Jewish leadership, who want to see him punished.

The assembly's accusations before Pilate are that Jesus is guilty of "subverting our nation," opposing the paying of taxes to Caesar, and claiming "to be Messiah, a king" (23:2). The reader knows these accusations to be mostly false. While the text clearly reveals Jesus as the Messiah, Jesus has certainly not subverted the nation. Instead, Jesus worked to keep his messianic identity mostly silent, silencing both demons and his own disciples from sharing that truth. He seems to have wanted people to come to that conclusion by themselves. And rather than opposing paying taxes to Caesar, Jesus was careful in his response to the bad-faith question about taxation, siding neither for or against the practice (20:25). These accusations ring in the reader's mind and help reveal the corrupt nature of the priesthood and their accusations, contrasted with Jesus's innocence. Pilate states clearly that Jesus is innocent in 23:4, saying, "I find no basis for a charge against this man." The people are insistent, saying that he stirs up the people in Galilee and Judea with his teaching (23:5). Again, these charges are not particularly true; although Jesus is a dynamic teacher with a challenging prophetic message that critiques the status quo, which gains him a significant following, there is no evidence in Luke of stirring up the people

---

13. Johnson, *Gospel of Luke*, 363. Parsons has a helpful discussion of the different understandings of these terms in scholarship and Luke's Gospel (*Luke*, 326–27).

14. Tacitus, *Ann.* 15.44.4; Josephus, *J.W.* 2.169–77; *Ant.* 18.35 §§55–62, 85–89; Philo, *Legat.* 299–305.

15. Bond, "Pontius Pilate," 679.

16. Bond, "Pontius Pilate."

Part 2: Initiation

in any harmful way. However, despite his insistence of Jesus's innocence, Pilate is caught between this and wanting to keep the peace with the leaders of the Jews. When he hears that Jesus is from Galilee, he seems to have a way out. In an attempt to abdicate responsibility for Jesus's trial, he sends him to Herod (23:7).

Herod is the leader in Galilee, as Pilate is in Judea. Our encounters with Herod so far in the Gospel have not been positive—he had John the Baptist killed (9:9) and might have sought to kill Jesus (13:31).[17] However, Herod appears curious about Jesus and wants to see him "perform a sign of some sort" (23:8). Jesus remains silent before Herod's questioning and gives him no answer (23:9). Once again, the "chief priests and teachers of the law" are present and "vehemently accusing him" (23:10). Jesus has no intention of doing a magic trick or arguing with those who falsely accuse him. As a result Herod joins in the ridicule by having Jesus dressed in a robe and sent back to Pilate, a clear move to mock both Jesus as the supposed "king of the Jews" and the Jewish people themselves. We once again see Luke's strategy of ekphrasis: we can picture an innocent Jesus, bruised and bloodied from the beatings, mockingly adorned in a purple robe. Luke notes that Herod and Pilate, once enemies, became friends after this (23:12). While there is no statement of innocence from Herod, Herod does not order him killed. (Pilate takes this as an assumption of innocence in 23:15.)

Back in Pilate's court, Pilate says again that the charges against Jesus have no basis (23:14) and he has done nothing to deserve death (23:15). He tries to release Jesus, but the crowd asks for Barabbas. While the leaders have been the clear instigators of the accusations against Jesus, this reference to the crowd asking for Barabbas is the only indication that there might have been a larger group. While both Matthew and Mark include the information that it was the chief priests and elders who persuaded the crowds to ask for Barabbas, Luke omits that point, as well as the statement that the crowd knew the chief priests were acting in self-interest in handing Jesus over.[18] This content seems to fit Luke's narrative, so it is unclear why Luke omitted it. Perhaps he felt the indictment of the chief priests had already been made plain by this point in the narrative. Additionally, there is

---

17. Johnson suggests that when the Pharisees warned Jesus that Herod was trying to kill him in 13:31, that must have been a lie, because Herod now has the reason and power to kill him but doesn't (*Gospel of Luke*, 368). However, since the Pharisees are conspicuously absent from the trial of Jesus, it seems strange for that to be a dramatic reveal here in the trial.

18. Matt 27:20; Mark 15:11.

no reference to Jesus being flogged in Luke beyond the guards beating him in 22:63–64. There is more great irony in that Barabbas, guilty of insurrection and murder—a fact Luke mentions twice (23:19, 25)—is released and Jesus is condemned to be crucified. Pilate again, for a fourth time, states he sees no reason for death.[19] There is a dramatic back-and-forth between Pilate and the crowd, with Luke presenting Pilate as persisting in trying to persuade them (23:18–24). Nonetheless, Pilate gives in to those who want Jesus crucified.

Original readers might have been familiar with trial scenes, as such scenes were common in Greco-Roman literature. Oftentimes the philosopher on trial would give long treatises or speeches in their final hours. Socrates is a famous example, who offers a stirring apology.[20] By stark contrast, Jesus says remarkably little. Even Paul in the latter part of Acts will be verbose in his own defense during his series of trials before numerous leaders. But Jesus, like the Suffering Servant of Isa 53:7, remains silent before his accusers. The readers of Luke have heard enough from Jesus to make their decision; his teachings and prophetic acts have been put on full display. From Luke's perspective the issue is clear.

CRUCIFIXION

Luke introduces a new character at the start of the march to Golgotha; a man named Simon is forced to carry the cross behind Jesus (Luke 23:26). Simon is a diasporic Jew from Cyrene, certainly in town for the Passover. This short little reference to Simon carrying the cross is important. By carrying the cross behind Jesus, Simon creates an ekphrastic picture of Jesus's words in 9:23 that "whoever wants to be my disciple must deny themselves and take up their cross daily and follow me." Johnson suggests, "Luke's wording unmistakably identifies this as an act of discipleship."[21] The reader recalls the high calling that is being a disciple of Jesus. So, the reader asks, where

---

19. I am of the opinion that Luke has Jesus declared innocent in Luke six times: four times by Pilate, once by the criminal crucified alongside Jesus, and once by the centurion at the foot of the cross. Some combine several of Pilate's declarations (Johnson, *Gospel of Luke*, 373) or see Herod's refusal to condemn Jesus as an additional one (Parsons, *Luke*, 330). Regardless of the number, the point remains: Luke overwhelmingly presents Jesus as innocent.

20. Johnson, *Gospel of Luke*, 366–67.

21. Johnson, *Gospel of Luke*, 374.

are his disciples? This detail again highlights the absence of Jesus's disciples in the ordeal; the hero is in the final battle alone, without his companions.

In addition to Simon, a large number of people follow him, including women who mourn and wail (23:27). Scholars disagree on the importance of these women,[22] but their mourning sets up Jesus's last statement of prophetic lament for Jerusalem. As in other apocalyptic teaching sections of Jesus in Luke, Jesus seems to describe the fall of Jerusalem to Rome in 70 CE. His final proverbial statement in 23:31—"For if people do these things when the tree is green, what will happen when it is dry?"—is debated.[23] However, given the recent emphasis on Jesus's innocence, his statement about the green and dry branches seems to be a statement about Rome's brutal treatment of Jesus, who was a nonviolent leader, compared with the even greater brutality with which Rome treats violent revolutions.[24]

Jesus makes his way outside the city to the place of the skull (23:33). While other hero stories see their heroes led to the belly of the beast, the belly of the whale, or ground zero, for Jesus it is a hill outside Jerusalem. Jesus's final battle will be one of self-giving and self-sacrifice. As N. T. Wright says,

> A new sort of power will be set loose upon the world, and it will be the power of self-giving love. This is the heart of the revolution that was launched on Good Friday. You cannot defeat the usual sort of power by the usual sort of means. If one force overcomes another, it is still "force" that wins. Rather at the heart of the victory of God over all the powers of the world there lies self-giving love, which, in obedience to the ancient prophetic vocation, will give its life "as a ransom for many."[25]

As Jesus is crucified, a few dramatic things happen. First, the people there mock him. Luke is careful to mention soldiers, the people, and the rulers all in some way participating in the mocking of and sneering at Jesus (23:35–39). The mocking of Jesus has been consistently present in Jesus's trials and crucifixion. The soldiers cast lots for his clothes, reminding the

---

22. For a good cross section of the opinions, see Bock, *Luke*, 2:1844–48.

23. Bock, *Luke*, 2:1847–48.

24. Bock disagrees, suggesting this "inserts Romans into a context where they are absent" (*Luke*, 2:1847). But Romans are clearly not absent here, for he agrees with most scholars that the apocalyptic words of Jesus here look ahead to the Roman conquest of Jerusalem in 70 CE. Bock sees this proverb as a statement of God's judgment on the people.

25. Wright, *Day the Revolution Began*, 222.

modern reader of the nakedness and the shame that come with crucifixion (23:34). Indeed, in the modern, Western world, Christians often consider the theological point that Jesus, the innocent sacrifice, takes away the guilt of our sin. However, Timothy Tennent, in his fascinating chapter on viewing the crucifixion through the shame-based culture of the East, reminds us that as the crucifixion is a public death, reserved for the worst criminals, public humiliation was a key element.[26] Jesus's innocence takes away our guilt; his public death also takes away our shame.

It is in this context, of the shameful death, with people casting lots for his clothes, that Jesus says perhaps the most remarkable thing in his final day: "Father, forgive, them for they do not know what they are doing."[27] We once again see Jesus demonstrate love and forgiveness for his enemies, as he did with the soldiers in the garden (22:51) and as he taught his disciples to pray (11:4). Our hero models what he teaches up to the final moment of affliction and death.

The mocking from the crowd has an ironic quality to it. The rulers say, "He saved others; let him save himself if he is God's Messiah, the Chosen One" (23:35). The soldiers, too, say similarly, "If you are the king of the Jews, save yourself" (23:37). While they are thinking specifically in terms of being saved in a physical sense, here specifically from crucifixion, Jesus predicted his own death and connected discipleship with carrying one's cross daily. He also predicted the persecution of those who followed him, which comes to pass in Acts. Thus, the comments of his accusers and mockers show their fundamental misunderstanding of Jesus and his mission. While to a Roman soldier and a condemned thief the ultimate salvation is merely avoiding premature physical death, Jesus has a different kind of salvation in mind.

Another accusation comes from one of the criminals crucified alongside Jesus, another dramatic feature of the crucifixion scene. These criminals (literally "evildoers" [Gk: κακοῦργοι]) demonstrate an important feature for Luke. We have seen how every group of people in Luke-Acts has some who respond positively to Jesus and others who do not. That

---

26. Tennent, "Anthropology."

27. The best and earliest manuscripts do not contain this saying of Jesus. While the external evidence suggests it is not original, there are numerous internal considerations arguing for inclusion, most compelling of which is Stephen's parallel statement in Acts 7:60 (alongside the other parallels between his and Jesus's deaths). Because of the numerous internal considerations, I am going to treat the saying as original for our narrative purposes here. For a fuller discussion, see Bock, *Luke*, 2:1867–68.

happens here as well. As one criminal mocks Jesus, urging him to save the criminals along with himself, the other criminal defends him. "We are punished justly, for we are getting what our deeds deserve. But this man has done nothing wrong" (23:41). Jesus is again pronounced innocent (for now the fifth time), contrasted with the guilty around him. Jesus assures this man that he will be in paradise "today" (23:43), a common word used with respect to salvation in Luke.[28] The call and influence of Jesus extend to all people, to every subgroup, regardless of past events. Luke demonstrates the wide attraction of Jesus and challenges the reader to consider how they would respond to the prophet.

JESUS'S DEATH

As the narrative shifts toward Jesus's death, two simultaneous events occur. Signs were common in the Greek world accompanying the death of a hero.[29] The first sign is a cosmic one; darkness comes over the whole land at noon (Luke 23:44). Bock suggests, "As the crucifixion proceeds, the heavens begin to comment."[30] While there seems to be literal darkness from this cosmic event—many scholars assume it was an eclipse—it may play a thematic role for Luke as well. Some have suggested it represents divine displeasure.[31] Conversely, Jesus had predicted that darkness reigns (22:53), and that is when the chief priests do their work. Indeed, the crucifixion of Jesus was orchestrated primarily by these chief priests, and their work is on full display. Regardless of the exact nature or meaning of the darkness, this odd weather event seems to give a cosmic dramatic import to the crucifixion of Jesus.[32]

---

28. Luke 2:11; 4:21; 5:26; 19:9–10.

29. Plutarch, *Romulus* 27.6; *Caesar* 69.4; Ovid, *Fast.* 2.493; Cicero, *Republic* 6.22; Pliny, *Natural History* 2.30. See also Bock, *Luke*, 2:1858.

30. Bock, *Luke*, 2:1858.

31. Parsons, *Luke*, 339.

32. Some have suggested that the darkness is metaphorical for God the Father being unable to look upon Jesus as he takes the sin of the world upon him. However, throughout both the Old and New Testaments, God regularly pursues relationship with humanity even though they are sinful. After Adam and Eve sin, God shows up to walk with them in the cool of the day. Likewise, as discussed in previous chapters, Jesus's ministry was largely focused on spending time with "sinners," drawing the critical eye of the Pharisees. Thus, that God is looking away from sin does not seem to be a valid explanation here.

The Ordeal

Second, Luke tells us that the curtain in the temple was torn in two (23:45). This is a significant event and is debated by scholars. Luke gives no explanation on what specifically this is to mean. Some suggest that some sort of judgment on the temple is intended, specifically that it will no longer be the dominant sacred symbol moving forward.[33] Others suggests that it is a sign that now all have access to God's presence, not only those with temple access.[34] Both of these ideas fit with the trajectory of Luke-Acts, for God's presence in Acts will be tied not to the temple but to the Holy Spirit, and all will be invited.[35]

After the occurrence of these signs, Jesus speaks for the final time, committing his spirit to his father and breaths his last, quoting Ps 31:5 (Ps 30 LXX). At this moment, a centurion, seeing what happened, declares Jesus innocent (23:47; Gk: δίκαιος), the sixth time Luke reminds us of this fact. While other Roman soldiers mock Jesus and gamble for his clothes, this one recognizes his innocence. Likewise, Luke tells us that the people who had gathered "beat their breasts" as they go away (23:48). These people would seem to be separate from the officials who mocked, and they represent the observing crowds who recognize the common grief that comes when Rome crucifies someone.

Two other groups are mentioned, those who knew him and the women (23:49). They stand at a distance, watching. It is unclear if the disciples are meant to be a part of this group or not, but the reader takes note that the women are witnesses of Jesus's death. As Luke begins to narrate Jesus's burial, a new character emerges named Joseph of Arimathea. There are two remarkable things about this character. First, Luke tells the reader he was a member of the council—the Sanhedrin—who did not consent to their decision (23:50–51). Thus, we learn a bit more about the trial and the proceedings that ended with Jesus being turned over to the Romans; it was not unanimous. Further, Joseph is concerned enough with the council's decision that he asks Pilate for Jesus's body and ensures he gets an honorable burial. Again here, as with rich people, Roman soldiers, and condemned thieves, even some from the council respond positively to Jesus, while others reject him.

---

33. Green, "Death of Jesus."
34. Parsons, *Luke*, 339.
35. For a fuller engagement with this event, see Fox, *Hermeneutics of Social Identity*, 136–37.

Second, Luke says that Joseph was waiting for the kingdom of God (23:51). This is similar language to how Luke describes Simeon and Anna when Jesus was presented in the temple in Luke 2. Luke has bookended Jesus's life—his dedication at the temple as a baby and his burial—with faithful Jews who are waiting for God's redemptive act in the world and who recognize Jesus as the one God sent. Despite all that we have seen in the ordeal, all the rejection the prophet has experienced, there remains a spark, a remnant who recognize Jesus for who he is.

The chapter ends with the women in focus once again. This group of faithful women who have traveled with Jesus from Galilee have observed his ministry (8:1–3), his death (23:49), and now his burial (23:55). They serve as the key forensic witnesses who can testify to what they have seen the entire way. And their story is not over.

And with that, the ordeal of our hero comes to a close. Jesus has entered the belly of the beast; he has made his self-sacrifice and accomplished what he came to do, what he predicted would happen.

But for this hero, the story does not end in a tomb.

DISCUSSION QUESTIONS

1. Did you notice anything new about the trials and crucifixion of Jesus while reading this chapter?
2. Does framing the betrayal and death of Jesus in heroic language change the experience for you in any way? How so?
3. When you think of your life journey, have you had an ordeal, a death of something that was like a climax?

PART 3

Return

Once the treasure has been grabbed, there is no reconciliation with the powers of the underworld . . . so there is a violent reaction of the whole unconscious system against the act, and the hero must escape.

—Joseph Campbell, *Pathways to Bliss*, 118

10

Resurrection

When the hero-quest has been accomplished . . . the adventurer must still return with his life-transmuting trophy . . . back into the kingdom of humanity, where the boon may redound to the renewing of the community, the nation, the planet, or the ten thousand worlds.
—Joseph Campbell, *The Hero with a Thousand Faces*, 193

Jesus appeared to them and said, "Peace be with you." They thought they were seeing a ghost and were scared half to death. He continued with them, "Don't be upset, and don't let all these doubting questions take over. Look at my hands; look at my feet—it's really me. Touch me. Look me over from head to toe. A ghost doesn't have muscle and bone like this." As he said this, he showed them his hands and feet. They still couldn't believe what they were seeing. It was too much; it seemed too good to be true.
—Luke 24:36b–40 MSG

AFTER THE ORDEAL, WHERE the hero encounters death, he must return with the spoils of the conquest, the boons to bestow upon humanity. Campbell talks about this as the "life-enhancing return" that completes the Hero's Journey.[1]

In the case of our hero, think how far we have come. It started with the angelic announcement to faithful Israel in the mundane world about the birth of a baby, with a call to adventure unlike any other. Next, we saw Jesus's miraculous birth and the marvelous songs creating expectations for the life of this promised one. The hero obtained supernatural aid at his baptism, before joining with companions and crossing the threshold into his road of trials. This led to a key moment of epiphany on the Mount of Transfiguration, commencing the journey to Jerusalem, where he will start his approach in the last week of his life. The week ends with the ordeal, the arrest, trial, and crucifixion of the hero.

This would be a remarkable story if it ended here. If this amazing life that brought healing and wisdom to so many ended with the tragic, unjust death of the hero, with that hero forgiving his enemies at the moment of his death, it would be one of the all-time great stories of martyrdom, sacrifice, and inspiration. But it would not be the story of Jesus.

Fleming Rutledge, in her seminal work on the crucifixion, puts it this way:

> *The crucifixion is the touchstone of Christian authenticity, the unique feature by which everything else, including the resurrection, is given its true significance.* The resurrection is not a set piece. It is not an isolated demonstration of divine dazzlement. It is not to be detached from its abhorrent first act. The resurrection is, precisely, the vindication of a man who was crucified. Without the cross at the center of the Christian proclamation, the Jesus story can be treated as just another story about a charismatic spiritual figure. It is the crucifixion that marks out Christianity as something definitively different in the history of religion. *It is in the crucifixion that the nature of God is truly revealed.* Since the resurrection is God's mighty transhistorical Yes to the historically crucified Son, we can assert that *the crucifixion is the most important historical event that has ever happened.* The resurrection, being a transhistorical event planted within history, does not cancel out the contradiction and shame of the cross in this present life; rather, the resurrection ratifies the cross as *the way* "until he comes."[2]

---

1. Campbell, *Hero with a Thousand Faces*, 35.
2. Rutledge, *Crucifixion*, 44; emphasis in original.

Resurrection

HOLY SATURDAY

As Rutledge suggests, we cannot fast-forward to the resurrection, skipping over the crucifixion; these events are forever linked. But within that linage is a void of space we would also do well not to overlook too quickly. Having traversed the ordeal of Good Friday, we cannot enter Easter Sunday until we have endured Holy Saturday. Alan Lewis says,

> The center of the drama itself is an empty-space. All the action and emotion, it seems, belong to two days only: despair and joy, dark and light, defeat and victory, the end and the beginning, evenly distributed in vivid contrast between what humanity did to Jesus on the first day and what God did for him on the third.[3]

Indeed, it may do us some good to ponder the plight of Peter, the sons of Zebedee, the rest of the Twelve, and the women on that Saturday. Although Luke tells us nothing about it, we can imagine the grief and perhaps even the fear they endured. Given the radical surprise that all experience on Sunday, Saturday certainly was not spent expectantly awaiting Sunday morning. It is more likely that, despite Jesus telling the disciples about his forthcoming death and resurrection (9:22; 18:33)—which they did not understand at the time—that they, too, did not have space in their theology for a crucified Messiah. They likely thought, despite all they had heard and seen, that Jesus was not the Messiah after all.[4]

Imagine their despair. They saw their friend, their rabbi, their Messiah, publicly executed. I imagine they spent Holy Saturday grieving. Weeping. Fearing that they might be next. Trying to figure out what to do with their lives now that what they had planned was over. Perhaps you have had a moment like that in your life; perhaps you can relate.

But that, dear reader, is not the end of our hero's story.

THE EMPTY TOMB

No, Jesus's story does not end with the cross, or with death, or even with Holy Saturday. But, indeed, it is at the tomb that our story continues, as the women who have followed Jesus from his early ministry days in Galilee

---

3. Lewis, *Between Cross and Resurrection*, 1.
4. We get a glimpse of this in 24:21 when the travelers on the road to Emmaus say, "We had hoped" that Jesus would redeem Israel, seemingly showing that they have abandoned those hopes.

seek to take spices to the body. These women had seen "the tomb and how his body was laid in it" (Luke 23:55). Remember that Jesus is killed on a Friday (23:54); the Sabbath starts at sundown on Friday and continues until sundown on Saturday. The women are not going to go to the cemetery after dark on Saturday, so they go first thing Sunday morning. This is the first reasonable opportunity they have to both keep the Sabbath—"But they rested on the Sabbath in obedience to the commandment" (23:56b)—and properly honor Jesus's body.

Arriving at the tomb, they do not find Jesus's body. While they are wondering about this—recall how often characters in Luke marvel or wonder—"two men in clothes that gleamed like lighting" appear (24:4). These men are later called angels, but Luke describes them here by their clothing. Parsons notes how the phrasing here, "suddenly, two men," occurs three times in Luke-Acts: the transfiguration (9:30), the resurrection (24:4), and the ascension (Acts 1:10).[5] At the three times in the narrative when the identity of Jesus as the true Son of God from heaven is most clear, two heavenly figures show up to commemorate it.

The words of the angels are a question and a statement: "Why do you look for the living among the dead? He is not here; he has risen! Remember how he told you, while he was still with you in Galilee: 'The Son of Man must be delivered over to the hands of sinners, be crucified and on the third day be raised again'" (24:6–7). As we noted in chapter 5, while the reader has been introduced to the women who were with Jesus in 8:1–3, it is here we find out that they have been with him *the whole time* as witnesses to his ministry, his death, and now his resurrection. They are charged to remember what he told them in 9:22, just after Peter's confession of Christ and just before the transfiguration. Jesus predicted the specifics of his death in 9:22, which started in motion the events that led up to this point. While this has been made somewhat plain to the reader, those living the events with the hero have failed to connect all the dots. At times the narrator has even told the reader that the disciples were unable to understand because the meaning was hidden from them (9:45; 18:34). Luke presents their experience with the risen Jesus as the key to deciphering things that have happened before; this will happen again in the post-resurrection narratives.

The women—now identified as Mary Magdalene, Joanna, Mary the mother of James, "and others," the first two being the same women mentioned by name in 8:1–3—rush off to tell the disciples (24:9). Proof is a

---

5. Parsons, *Luke*, 155.

common motif in hero stories; when the hero has traveled to another world and come back, "not being believed is a perennial problem."[6] Here it is not Jesus himself who is not believed but the testimony of the women. However, disbelief will be a common occurrence in Luke's resurrection narratives. The reason for disbelief is made clear: it is not because of a paucity of evidence or because of unreliable messengers but because of the grandeur and astounding nature of the event.[7] This serves to highlight how completely disillusioned the disciples were between the death and resurrection but also the absolute heavenly joy they experience at the resurrection, so much so that they hesitate to believe it. It is also consistent with their lack of understanding in the ministry of Jesus (9:45; 18:34). When the women tell the disciples, Peter runs to the tomb to see for himself, finding the tomb empty and only the bedclothes remaining. This leaves Peter in a state of wonder.[8]

THE ROAD TO EMMAUS

The scene then shifts to a different location but on the same day. Two disciples, Cleopas and an unnamed disciple, are walking along the road north of Jerusalem. The risen Jesus himself approaches them on the road, but they are kept from recognizing him (Luke 24:16).[9] Hero stories typically present the hero having gone through some sort of significant change. Typically this is a moral change or intellectual change, after their having faced a personal fear. For Jesus, his change is not moral or intellectual, but the very nature of his existence seems to be different. Campbell talks about the hero being "the master of two worlds" after achieving victory; that is what we witness here.[10] Jesus still has his human body, but it is now in its glorified state. When they do recognize Jesus in 24:31, he will disappear from their sight. Later he seems to appear while they are marveling about his resurrection (24:36). While this may lead the reader to think that the resurrection was primarily spiritual in nature, in the realm of visions or dreams, Luke makes clear that this is categorically not the case. The tomb is empty; Jesus's

---

6. Vogler, *Writer's Journey*, 241.
7. Johnson, *Gospel of Luke*, 391.
8. Recall that this word is common in Luke for wondrous events, as in 1:21, 63; 2:18, 33; 4:22; 7:9; 8:25; 11:14, 38; 20:26 (Johnson, *Gospel of Luke*, 389).
9. Again, reminiscent of 9:45 and 18:34, where they were kept from understanding.
10. Campbell, *Hero with a Thousand Faces*, 229–37.

physical body is not in there. Further, Jesus demonstrates that he is not a ghost but is flesh and bones, can be touched, and even eats food (24:37–43). Thus, he is the master of two worlds, but the nature of change that Jesus has gone through is of a different order than human heroes. Jesus was the prophet, who had a special identity as the true Son of God, imbued with supernatural aid from the Holy Spirit to work miracles; now he is different, glorified, and even more spectacular. Jesus's risen state is his glorified state.

The travelers on the road to Emmaus capture the magnitude of the story of Jesus. Remember, Luke wants to set the coming of Jesus in the time and space of the real world, and that includes Jerusalem and the people there at a particular time and place. "Are you the only one visiting Jerusalem who does not know the things that have happened there in these days?" Cleopas asks (24:18). Jesus appears to be like Merlin or Gandalf here, a wise sage who plays dumb for the purpose of teaching. Additionally, the concept of the gods disguising themselves among humans was common for ancient readers.[11] The two travelers reply, giving the perfect Lukan summary of Jesus and his ministry: "He was a prophet, powerful in word and deed before God and all the people. The chief priests and our rulers handed him over to be sentenced to death, and they crucified him; but we had hoped that he was the one who was going to redeem Israel. And what is more, it is the third day since all this took place" (24:19b–21). The reader again sees the disillusionment in the disciples with their statement "we had hoped he was the one to redeem Israel." This hope of the liberation of Israel was introduced by Luke early, as far back as the birth narratives.[12] Yet they assume redemption has not happened. In their minds, even with the hints of resurrection, the crucifixion was a defeat, a failure, an end of the saving narrative of Jesus.

The irony is thick. Two disciples[13] of Jesus do not recognize him and explain to him what has happened to Jesus the last few days. They have presumably been with him the whole time, present for his multiple predictions of his death and resurrection on the third day. They have heard testimony from some women and others that the tomb is empty. Despite all this, they remain disillusioned and in the dark regarding what has really happened, as they converse with the one who truly knows the full cosmic extent of what

---

11. Parsons, *Luke*, 349.

12. See Luke 1:68 and 2:38 (Johnson, *Gospel of Luke*, 394).

13. These are apparently not part of "the Twelve," but seemingly part of the larger community of disciples surrounding Jesus.

happened. This is the reason for Jesus's statement, which may sound harsh: "How foolish you are, and how slow to believe all that the prophets have spoken!" (24:25).[14] In our culture, we might say, "Are you blind?," a rhetorical question to highlight the obvious nature of something. The reader is on the inside with Jesus, while these two disciples remain on the outside, failing to understand.

Jesus, the wise sage playing dumb for teaching purposes, now speaks and explains the Scriptures, beginning from "Moses and all the prophets" (24:27). What do you suppose Jesus taught them? While the reader may be intensely curious to hear what Jesus says regarding how the Hebrew Scriptures speak of him and the ordeal, Luke may give us a glimpse of that content in Acts 7 and 13, where Stephen and Paul, respectively, tell the story of redemption history, starting with Israel and tracing it through the story of Jesus. Luke has no intention of planting a seed about Jesus's roots in Israel's history and then leaving the reader in the dark. Indeed, much of this groundwork has already been laid in the canticles and the ministry of Jesus.

The two disciples are intrigued and invite Jesus, still unrecognizable to them, to eat with them. Jesus takes bread, gives thanks, breaks it, and gives it to them, at which point "their eyes were opened and they recognized him" (24:31). Again we see that it is experience with the risen Jesus that is the key to fully understanding. They share their suspicions when they say, "Were not our hearts burning within us while he talked with us on the road and opened the Scriptures to us?" (24:32).

This language where Jesus takes, gives thanks, breaks, and gives bread is an important linguistic key for Luke. As with the "two men" language above, so there are three scenes that all use extremely similar language: the feeding of the five thousand (Luke 9:10–17), the Last Supper (22:19), and here. We have three scenes, each in a different sphere of Jesus's work (Galilee, Jerusalem, and resurrected state), each coming near a climactic moment, connected via very similar language.[15] The scenes serve to give an internal connectedness between these three divisions of Jesus's ministry and to highlight the importance of shared meals, a feature that will continue into Acts.

---

14. Johnson notes how these words were often used by philosophers for those without understanding (*Gospel of Luke*, 395).

15. Parsons, *Luke*, 149–50.

PART 3: RETURN

JESUS APPEARS TO THE DISCIPLES

As the two travelers on the road to Emmaus return to Jerusalem, they tell the Eleven about their experience with Jesus (Luke 24:33–35).[16] As they are discussing this, "Jesus himself stood among them and said to them, 'Peace be with you'" (24:36). This is the third resurrection scene of Jesus. At his appearance, the disciples think he is a ghost.[17] Jesus presents the physical nature of his existence to the disciples so they can understand—he has flesh and bone, he can be touched, he is a physical being. He even asks for food (broiled fish) and eats (24:42–43). This is now the second resurrection appearance in a row where Jesus shares a meal with his followers as a significant part of the encounter.[18] Meals have played an important role in Luke, with Jesus using them to include outsiders, teach, and cast a vision of his eschatological kingdom. Parsons suggests that there are two "Last Suppers" in Luke, the first on the night he was betrayed and this one with his disciples after the resurrection.[19]

It is at this meal that Jesus says to them, "This is what I told you while I was still with you: Everything must be fulfilled that is written about me in the Law of Moses, the Prophets and the Psalms" (24:44). Luke then says that he opened their minds so they could understand the Scriptures (24:45). Once again, it is experience with the resurrected Jesus that makes everything that came before make sense. The triumph of the hero gives the story that comes before fuller meaning. While the previous story is not devoid of meaning without the end, we must have the conclusion of the story for the rest of it to have full significance. In this way, it is somewhat like a movie or novel that has a surprise ending—*The Sixth Sense* comes to mind.[20] While there were clues of the nature of the ending the whole time, the reveal at the end makes you want to rewatch the movie, looking for what you missed. While Luke shows Jesus explicitly predicting his death

---

16. The text seems to suggest that Jesus appeared to Peter off camera in 24:34. However, some, including some of the earliest interpreters, understood that Simon Peter was the second traveler on the road to Emmaus. See Parsons, *Luke*, 352.

17. The Greek here is πνεῦμα (spirit), as opposed to the other word that is used when Jesus is walking on the water in Matt 14:26 and Mark 6:49 and think he is a ghost (φάντασμά). The point is that Jesus is not a spirit but has flesh and bone.

18. Parsons notes how the language here suggests more of a mutual eating than only Jesus eating to demonstrate his physical nature (*Luke*, 353).

19. Parsons, *Luke*, 354–55.

20. Shyamalan, *Sixth Sense*.

and resurrection, the end is so remarkable that the earlier parts of the story deserve another look.

Jesus reminds them again as he did numerous times before: "This is what is written: The Messiah will suffer and rise from the dead on the third day" (24:46). And at this point we start to see a shift towards Acts. Jesus asserts that "repentance for the forgiveness of sins will be preached in his name to all nations, beginning at Jerusalem. You are witnesses of these things. I am going to send you what my Father has promised; but stay in the city until you have been clothed with power from on high" (24:47-49). This is a precursor to the events that will occur in Acts 1:3-8. Jesus lays out the basic themes of the apostolic mission in Acts—repentance, forgiveness of sins, and the disciples as witnesses, all starting in Jerusalem.[21] But before that happens, they will be clothed with power from on high, the Holy Spirit, their own experience of receiving supernatural aid, much like at Jesus's baptism.

ASCENSION

The Gospel of Luke ends with the ascension of Jesus, where he is taken up into heaven. Luke has prepared the reader for this eventuality, with Jesus discussing his exodus with Moses and Elijah in glory on the Mount of Transfiguration (Luke 9:30-31) and the journey to Jerusalem commencing with an eye towards his time "to be taken up to heaven" (9:51). The reader now sees the culmination of those prognostications: "The narrative has prepared us for this departure and for its prophetic significance."[22]

One of the last things Jesus does in the Gospel of Luke is bless the disciples. The Gospel of Luke opened with a priest, Zechariah, in the temple. It would be customary for him to speak a blessing over people after the ceremony in the temple; he cannot because he is not able to speak.[23] Mekkattukunnel argues that Jesus himself, in his teaching and healing ministry, has been the blessing in the Gospel of Luke.[24] In addition, the blessing of Jesus at the end, doing what Zechariah could not do, forms an *inclusio* that

---

21. Johnson, *Gospel of Luke*, 405.
22. Johnson, *Gospel of Luke*, 406.
23. Mekkattukunnel, *Priestly Blessing*, 197.
24. Mekkattukunnel, *Priestly Blessing*, 221-22. He also argues that this presents Jesus as the true high priest (171-87).

PART 3: RETURN

encompasses the entire Gospel.[25] The disciples will carry forward the important work that Jesus started, as the successors of Moses and Elijah did.[26]

After Jesus leaves, the disciples worship Jesus, returning to Jerusalem with great joy, regularly going to the temple (24:52–53). And so our narrative ends where it began, with spiritual activity happening in the temple. Where the angel told Zechariah his prayer was answered, the disciples stay continually praising God. The hero has triumphed, and evil has been vanquished, at least for the time being.

CONCLUSION

While the conflict of Jesus with the powers and the arrest and crucifixion of Jesus needed significant exposition, taking more than four chapters and including the declaration of Jesus as innocent multiple times, the resurrection is more obvious. It needs less explanation and exposition. The reader has been privy to the eventual trajectory the whole time, on the inside, even when Jesus's closest disciples remain on the outside.

The reader is left to decide how they will respond to the prophet. Luke has masterfully pulled the reader along on this hero quest. Although the hero experienced the ordeal, it was not the end of the story. Indeed, the hero has returned, having conquered death and giving boons to mankind, in the form of insight, forgiveness of sins, and blessing to his followers. These boons will be elaborated on more in Acts. In some ways, the story is just beginning. The stage is set for the sequel.

DISCUSSION QUESTIONS

1. What do you think the experience was like for Jesus's disciples, the women, and his other friends and family on Holy Saturday?
2. What do you think the significance is of the reader knowing and remembering Jesus's predictions of his death and resurrection but his disciples all forgetting?
3. What examples can you think of from life, movies, novels, etc. that contained a significant return or resurrection that was significant for you?

---

25. Parsons, *Departure of Jesus*, 69–81, 109–11.
26. Johnson, *Gospel of Luke*, 406.

Resurrection

Bibliography

Alter, Robert. *The Art of Biblical Narrative*. New York: Basic, 2011.
Athas, George. *Bridging the Testaments: The History and Theology of God's People in the Second Temple Period*. Grand Rapids: Zondervan Academic, 2023.
Baden, Joel S. "The Nature of Barrenness in the Hebrew Bible." In *Disability Studies and Biblical Literature*, edited by Candida R. Moss and Jeremy Schipper, 13–27. Basingstoke: Palgrave Macmillan, 2011.
Bancks, Tristan. "Beyond the Hero's Journey: 'Joseph [Campbell] is my Yoda.'—George Lucas (1)." *Australian Screen Education* 33 (2003) 32–34.
Beers, Holly. *The Followers of Jesus as the "Servant": Luke's Model from Isaiah for the Disciples in Luke-Acts*. LNTS 535. London: Bloomsbury T&T Clark, 2015.
Bilezikian, Gilbert G. *The Liberated Gospel: A Comparison of the Gospel of Mark and a Greek Tragedy*. Eugene, OR: Wipf and Stock, 1977.
Blomberg, Craig L. *Jesus and the Gospels: An Introduction and Survey*. 3rd ed. Nashville: B&H Academic, 2022.
Bock, Darrell L. *Luke*. 2 vols. BECNT. Grand Rapids: Baker Academic, 1996.
Bock, Darrell L., and J. Ed Komoszewski, eds. *Jesus, Skepticism, and the Problem of History: Criteria and Context in the Study of Christian Origins*. Grand Rapids: Zondervan, 2019.
Bond, H. K. "Pontius Pilate." In *Dictionary of Jesus and the Gospels*, edited by Joel B. Green et al., 679–80. 2nd ed. IVP Bible Dictionary. Downers Grove, IL: InterVarsity, 2013.
Booker, Christopher. *The Seven Basic Plots: Why We Tell Stories*. London: Bloomsbury, 2004.
Brown, Jeannine K. *The Gospels as Stories: A Narrative Approach to Matthew, Mark, Luke, and John*. Grand Rapids: Baker Academic, 2020.
———. "Reconstructing the Historical Pharisees: Does Matthew's Gospels Have Anything to Contribute?" In *Jesus, Skepticism, and the Problem of History: Criteria and Context in the Study of Christian Origins*, edited by Darrell L. Bock and J. Ed Komoszewski, 164–82. Grand Rapids: Zondervan Academic, 2019.
Brown, Jeannine K., and Kyle Roberts. "Reading Judaism Ethically in the Post-Holocaust Era." In *Matthew*, 506–22. Two Horizons New Testament Commentary. Grand Rapids: Eerdmans, 2018.
Brown, Raymond E. *The Birth of the Messiah: A Commentary on the Infancy Narratives in the Gospels of Matthew and Luke*. AYBRL. New Haven, CT: Yale University Press, 1999.

Bibliography

Burge, Gary M., and Gene L. Green. *The New Testament in Antiquity: A Survey of the New Testament Within Its Cultural Contexts*. 2nd ed. Grand Rapids: Zondervan Academic, 2020.

Campbell, Joseph. *The Hero with a Thousand Faces*. 2nd ed. Princeton: Princeton University Press, 1968.

———. *Myths to Live By*. New York: Penguin, 1972.

———. *Pathways to Bliss: Mythology and Personal Transformation*. Novato, CA: New World Library, 2013.

———. *The Power of Myth*. With Bill Moyers. New York: Anchor, 1991.

———. *Thou Art That: Transforming Religious Metaphor*. Novato, CA: New World Library, 2013.

Collins, John J. *The Apocalyptic Imagination: An Introduction to Jewish Apocalyptic Literature*. Grand Rapids: Eerdmans, 2016.

Dionysius of Halicarnassus. *Roman Antiquities*. Translated by Earnest Cary. 7 vols. LCL. Cambridge: Harvard University Press, 1937.

Doty, William G. "Myth Around the Clock: From Mama Myth to Mythographic Analysis." In *Mythography: The Study of Myths and Rituals*, 3–30. 2nd ed. Tuscaloosa: University of Alabama Press, 2000.

Downs, David J. "Economics." In *Dictionary of Jesus and the Gospels*, edited by Joel B. Green et al., 219–26. 2nd ed. IVP Bible Dictionary. Downers Grove, IL: InterVarsity, 2013.

———. "Economics, Taxes, and Tithes." In *The World of the New Testament: Social, Cultural, and Historical Contexts*, edited by Joel B. Green and Lee Martin McDonald, 156–68. Grand Rapids: Baker Academic, 2017.

Fee, Gordon D., and Douglas Stuart. *How to Read the Bible for All It's Worth*. 4th ed. Grand Rapids: Zondervan, 2014.

Fitzmyer, Joseph. *The Gospel According to Luke I–IX*. AB 28. Garden City, NY: Doubleday, 1981.

———. *The Gospel According to Luke X–XXIV*. AB 28A. Garden City, NY: Doubleday, 1985.

Fox, Nickolas A. *The Hermeneutics of Social Identity in Luke-Acts*. Eugene, OR: Pickwick, 2021.

———. "Storytelling Sequels: Multi-volume Mysteries in Luke-Acts and the Original Series of *Twin Peaks*." In *Theology, Religion, and Twin Peaks*, edited by John Anthony Dunne and Kris Song. Lanham, MD: Lexington, forthcoming.

Fredriksen, Paula. "Did Jesus Oppose the Purity Laws?" *BRev* 11 (1995) 18–25, 42–47.

———. "What You See Is What you Get: Context and Content in Current Research on the Historical Jesus." *ThTo* 52 (1995) 75–97.

Gorman, Michael J. *Reading Revelation Responsibly: Uncivil Worship and Witness: Following the Lamb into the New Creation*. Eugene, OR: Cascade, 2010.

Gottschall, Jonathan. *The Storytelling Animal: How Stories Make us Human*. New York: HarperCollins, 2012.

Green, Joel B. "The Death of Jesus and the Rending of the Temple Veil (Luke 23:44–49): A Window into Luke's Understanding of Jesus and the Temple." In *Society of Biblical Literature 1991 Seminar Papers*, edited by E. A. Lovering Jr., 543–57. SBLSPS 30. Atlanta: Scholars, 1991.

———. *The Gospel of Luke*. NICNT. Grand Rapids: Eerdmans, 1997.

Bibliography

Hanson, K. C., and Douglas E. Oakman. *Palestine in the Time of Jesus: Social Structures and Social Conflicts.* 2nd ed. Minneapolis: Fortress, 2008.

Hanson, Paul D. *The Dawn of Apocalyptic: The Historical and Sociological Roots of Jewish Apocalyptic Theology.* Philadelphia: Fortress, 1975.

Heard, W. J., and K. Yamazaki-Ransom. "Revolutionary Movements." In *Dictionary of Jesus and the Gospels,* edited by Joel B. Green et al., 789–99. 2nd ed. IVP Bible Dictionary. Downers Grove, IL: InterVarsity, 2013.

Helyer, Larry R. "The Hasmoneans and the Hasmonean Era." In *The World of the New Testament: Social, Cultural, and Historical Contexts,* edited by Joel B. Green and Lee Martin McDonald, 38–53. Grand Rapids: Baker Academic, 2017.

Hermogenes. "On Ecphrasis." In *Progymnasmata: Greek Textbooks of Prose Composition and Rhetoric,* edited and translated by George Kennedy, 86–87. WGRW 10. Leiden: Brill, 2003.

Heschel, Abraham Joshua. *The Prophets.* New York: HarperCollins, 1962.

Horsley, Richard A. *Bandits, Prophets, and Messiahs: Popular Movements in the Time of Jesus.* With John S. Hanson. Harrisburg, PA: Trinity International, 1999.

———. *Revolt of the Scribes: Resistance and Apocalyptic Origins.* Minneapolis: Fortress, 2010.

Jeremias, Joachim. *Jerusalem in the Time of Jesus: An Investigation into Economic and Social Conditions During New Testament Period.* Philadelphia: Fortress, 1969.

Johns, Cheryl Bridges. *Re-Enchanting the Text: Discovering the Bible as Sacred, Dangerous, and Mysterious.* Grand Rapids: Baker Academic, 2023.

Johnson, Luke Timothy. *The Gospel of Luke.* Edited by Daniel J. Harrington. SP 3. Collegeville, MN: Liturgical, 2006.

Jung, Carl. *The Archetypes of the Collective Unconscious.* Translated by R. F. C. Hull. New York: Bollingen, 1969.

Kierkegaard, Søren. *The Sickness unto Death.* Translated by Walter Lowrie. Princeton: Princeton University Press, 1941.

Kinman, Brent. "Jesus' 'Triumphal Entry' in Light of Pilate's." *NTS* 40 (1992) 442–48.

———. "Parousia, Jesus' 'A-Triumphal' Entry, and the Fate of Jerusalem (Luke 19:28–44)." *JBL* 118 (1999) 279–94.

Lee-Barnewall, Michelle. "Pharisees, Sadducees, and Essenes." In *The World of the New Testament: Social, Cultural, and Historical Contexts,* edited by Joel B. Green and Lee Martin McDonald, 217–27. Grand Rapids: Baker Academic, 2017.

Levine, Amy-Jill. "Discharging Responsibility: Matthean Jesus, Biblical Law, and Hemorrhaging Woman." In *A Feminist Companion to Matthew,* edited by Amy-Jill Levine with Marianne Blickenstaff, 70–87. Feminist Companion to the New Testament and Early Christian Writings. Sheffield: Sheffield Academic, 2001.

Lewis, Alan E. *Between Cross and Resurrection: A Theology of Holy Saturday.* Grand Rapids: Eerdmans, 2001.

Liu, James H., and Janos László. "A Narrative Theory of History and Identity." In *Social Representations and Identity: Content, Process, and Power,* edited by Gail Moloney and Iain Walker, 85–107. New York: Palgrave McMillan, 2007.

Livy. *The Early History of Rome.* Translated by Aubrey de Sélincourt. London: Penguin, 1960.

Lucas, George, dir. *A New Hope.* Part 4 of *Star Wars.* 1977; Lucasfilm, 2013. DVD.

Lundin, Roger, et al. *The Promise of Hermeneutics.* Grand Rapids: Eerdmans, 1999.

Bibliography

Mason, Steve. "Josephus's Pharisees." In *The Pharisees*, edited by Joseph Sievers and Amy-Jill Levine, 80–111. Grand Rapids: Eerdmans, 2021.

Mekkattukunnel, Andrews George. *The Priestly Blessing of the Risen Christ: An Exegetico-Theological Analysis of Luke 24, 50–53*. European University Studies 714. Bern: Lang, 2001.

Milne, B. A. "Judgment." In *New Bible Dictionary*, edited by I. Howard Marshall et al., 631–34. 3rd ed. New Bible Set. Downers Grove, IL: IVP Academic, 1996.

Moyers, Bill, host. *Joseph Campbell and the Power of Myth*. Aired June 21–26, 1988, on PBS. https://www.pbs.org/show/joseph-campbell-and-the-power-of-myth-with-bill-moyers/.

Murdock, Maureen. *The Heroine's Journey: Woman's Quest for Wholeness*. Boulder, CO: Shambhala, 1990.

Nolland, John. *Luke 1:1—9:20*. WBC 35A. Nashville: Nelson, 2000.

Osborne, Grant. *Revelation*. BECNT. Grand Rapids: Baker Academic, 2002.

Pao, David. *Acts and the Isaianic New Exodus*. Grand Rapids: Baker Academic, 2000.

Parsons, Mikeal C. *The Departure of Jesus in Luke-Acts: The Ascension Narratives in Context*. JSNTSup 21. Sheffield: JSOT, 1987.

———. *Luke*. Paideia. Grand Rapids: Baker Academic, 2015.

Peterson, Eugene H. *Reversed Thunder: The Revelation of John and the Praying Imagination*. San Francisco: HarperOne, 1991.

Pitre, Brant. "Apocalypticism and Apocalyptic Teaching." In *Dictionary of Jesus and the Gospels*, edited by Joel B. Green et al., 23–33. 2nd ed. IVP Bible Dictionary. Downers Grove, IL: InterVarsity, 2013.

Resseguie, James L. *Narrative Criticism of the New Testament: An Introduction*. Grand Rapids: Baker Academic, 2005.

Rhoads, David, et al. *Mark as Story: An Introduction to the Narrative of a Gospel*. 3rd ed. Minneapolis: Fortress, 2012.

Rothfuss, Patrick. *The Wise Man's Fear*. London: Gollancz, 2012.

Rowland, Christopher. *The Open Heaven: The Study of Apocalyptic in Judaism and Early Christianity*. New York: Crossroad, 1982.

Rutledge, Fleming. *The Crucifixion: Understanding the Death of Jesus Christ*. Grand Rapids: Eerdmans, 2015.

Sanders, Jack T. "The Parable of the Pounds and Lucan Anti-Semitism." TS 42 (1981) 660–68.

Shklovsky, Victor. "Art as Technique." In *Russian Formalist Criticism: Four Essays*, translated by Lee T. Lemon and Marion J. Reis, 3–24. Lincoln: University of Nebraska Press, 1965.

Shyamalan, M. Night. *The Sixth Sense*. Burbank: Buena Vista, 1999.

Siegel, Daniel J. *Mindsight: The New Science of Personal Transformation*. New York: Bantam, 2010.

Sievers, Joseph, and Amy-Jill Levine, eds. *The Pharisees*. Grand Rapids: Eerdmans, 2021.

Simpson, William, dir. *Myths and Monsters*. Episode 1, "Heroes and Villains." Aired Dec. 23, 2017, on Netflix.

Snodgrass, Klyne. *Stories with Intent: A Comprehensive Guide to the Parables of Jesus*. Grand Rapids: Eerdmans, 2018.

Soloponte, Neal. *The Ultimate Hero's Journey: 195 Essential Plot Stages Found in the Best Novels & Movies*. Berlin: Tango and Blum, 2017.

Bibliography

Steele, E. Springs. "Luke 11:37–54—A Modified Hellenistic Symposium?" *JBL* 103 (1984) 379–94.

Storr, Will. *The Science of Storytelling: Why Stories Make Us Human and How to Tell Them Better.* New York: Abrams, 2021.

Strauss, Mark L. "Sadducees." In *Dictionary of Jesus and the Gospels*, edited by Joel B. Green et al., 823–25. 2nd ed. IVP Bible Dictionary. Downers Grove, IL: InterVarsity, 2013.

Sweet, Leonard, et al. *A is for Abductive: The Language of the Emerging Church.* Grand Rapids: Zondervan, 2003.

Tannehill, Robert. *The Gospel According to Luke.* Vol. 1 of *The Narrative Unity of Luke-Acts: A Literary Interpretation.* Philadelphia: Fortress, 1986.

Taylor, Charles. *A Secular Age.* Cambridge, MA: Belknap, 2007.

Tennent, Timothy C. "Anthropology: Human Identity in Shame-Based Cultures of the Far East." In *Theology in the Context of World Christianity: How the Global Church Is Influencing the Way We Think About and Discuss Theology*, 77–104. Grand Rapids: Zondervan, 2007.

Thiessen, Matthew. *Jesus and the Forces of Death: The Gospels' Portrayal of Ritual Impurity Within First-Century Judaism.* Grand Rapids: Baker Academic, 2020.

Truby, John. *The Anatomy of Story: 22 Steps to Becoming a Master Storyteller.* New York: Farrer, Straus, and Giroux, 2007.

Vogler, Christopher. *The Writer's Journey: Mythic Structure for Writers.* 25th anniv. ed. Studio City: Wiese, 2020.

The Wachowski Brothers, dirs. *The Matrix.* 1999; Warner Brothers, 2004. DVD.

Wright, N. T. *The Day the Revolution Began: Reconsidering the Meaning of Jesus's Crucifixion.* New York: HarperCollins, 2016.

www.ingramcontent.com/pod-product-compliance
Lightning Source LLC
Chambersburg PA
CBHW031500160426
43195CB00010BB/1042